From Fizzle to Sizzle

Four Crucial Tools for Relationship Repair

Dr. Caron Goode, NCC

Dr. Minette Riordan, CPC

Scissortail Publishing

From Fizzle to Sizzle: Four Crucial Tools for Relationship Repair

ISBN-13: 978-0-61572-459-1

Published by Scissortail Publishing

7527 Padova Drive

Goleta, CA 93117

Cover Design by Marty Yochum Casey

Limits of Liability and Disclaimer of Warranty

The purpose of this book is to educate and entertain. The authors and/or publisher and/or editor shall have neither liability nor responsibility for any loss or damage caused, or alleged to be caused, directly or indirectly by the information contained in this book.

If you have major life issues like insatiable neediness, a sexual disorder or addiction, or attention issues that make you incapable of taking the simple steps outlined in these pages, this book won't work for you. Instead, seek help from a health professional, mental health consultant or therapist.

Praise for the Power of "From Fizzle to Sizzle"

"The ability to build and maintain positive, healthy and productive relationships is essential in every area of life. *From Fizzle to Sizzle* provides proven skills and relevant examples to help you have some 'ah-ha!' moments. The result? More fulfillment. More love. More connection. A must-read for anyone who is feeling the stress and burden of a relationship that has fizzled!"

- **Mindy Audlin**, CEO of Network on Purpose and author of *What If It All Goes Right?: Creating a New World of Peace, Prosperity & Possibility*

Dr. Goode and Dr. Riordan have struck gold in *From Fizzle to Sizzle: 4 Crucial Tools for Relationship Repair*. They have identified the key areas where any relationship can go off the tracks and have offered tools to keep all of your relationships humming along a healthy path of connection. This book is for those of you who have felt something was missing in other relationship books. It hits the mark on every level."

- **Dr. Tina Ferguson, Ph.D.**, Author of *The Power of Love* and *Must Be Present to Win*

"*From Fizzle to Sizzle* is a very timely and enlightening book to help jump start any relationship that has become stagnant or challenged. Today's stresses can pose a strain on anyone juggling love and life. Relating to significant others and still being present for all the people we are to everyone in our lives is draining, yet we can learn to balance out all those needs and responsibilities and manage our love relationship in easy steps that bring back the sizzle. No more dull, lack of lust in our love lives thanks to Riordan and Goode."

- **Katherine (Kat) Smith**, Loveologist and Author of *Romantic Retreats in Texas*

"Whether your relationship is with a lover, your parent, a child, or co-worker, this book will invariably stretch you beyond your comfort zone and offer opportunities for sharing, learning, and managing life together. In *From Fizzle to Sizzle* the authors show how to identify your needs and values and be crystal clear about what you want in your relationships. With four crucial tools—core temperaments, values, emotional hijacking, and HUG — this book shares the secrets to relationship repair. Develop (or repair) a relationship as you learn why people act as they do, how to respond to them, and how to stay true to your own values."

- **Yvonne Perry**, Author of *Whose Stuff Is This? ~ Finding Freedom from the Thoughts, Feelings, and Energy of Those Around You*

"*From Fizzle to Sizzle* fulfills an urgent social need in teaching readers how to develop relationship skills in a high tech world. The well-informed authors clearly explain how being hardwired for relationships creates conflict when communication falters because of expectations. While the book is geared towards the self-awareness the reader takes into personal relationships, I think there is also a great deal of application to professional relationships as well. Making a commitment to becoming real, authentic and staying true to one's values enhances our ability to successfully build relationships both personally and professionally. An easy and enjoyable read!"

- **Darlene Ellison**, M.S. Author, *The Predator Next Door*

"An important key in avoiding the most common decision-making traps is the ability to really understand your values and what's important to you. In From Fizzle to Sizzle, Dr. Caron Goode and Dr. Minette Riordan help readers understand their own values and to effectively listen so that they can identify the values of others in their relationships. Readers learn the four crucial tools in understanding how to act and react in healthy ways so that they can make values-based decisions in relationships. It's a great read and a useful resource."

Traci Shoblom, Senior Partner, Decision Systems International

"*From Fizzle to Sizzle* digs deep into values and other components through relatable examples and innovative, easy-to-do practices. I especially like the step-by-step approach to identifying characteristics and applying them to relationships. Dr. Caron Goode and Dr. Minette Riordan offer a fresh way to describe four well-named 'types' and encourage readers create their own composite descriptions—brilliant!"

– **Barbara McNichol,** nonfiction book editor and author of *Word Trippers*

From *Fizzle to Sizzle* is one of the best books I've read on how to truly establish whole relationships in one's life. It is a must read for all ages whether you're starting the journey and taking proactive steps to establish real and meaningful relationships in your life or you are in the process of bringing healing and repair to your present ones. The authors take you through simple action steps to develop healthy relationships in all areas of your life whether it's your marriage, your relationship with your child or those in your profession. Bring the sizzle back into your life and relationships by investing in this book and using the powerful wisdom shared by Dr. Goode and Dr. Riordan.

- **Lesa Day,** Parenting Family Coach and author of *The Yes I Can Child*

Dedication

To all of the men and women who live to love and love to be in relationships.
To all those lovers, parents, and friends who have been hurt, and healed, and moved forward with courage to fill their hearts and lives with rich relationships.

To Dr. Tom Goode, the love of my lives, who taught me that relationship is commitment to respect, responsiveness, acceptance, being present, loving someone enough to be honest, and wanting our gifts to serve those called to be in relationships also.

To Brad Dobson, my husband and life partner, for his unconditional love and faith in me, for always being there, for being a hopeless romantic and reminding me that romance is an integral part of every relationship. And to my two amazing children, Conner and Maggie, for their patience and support. They are beautiful souls who enlighten and engage me every day.

We also want to extend a heartfelt thank you to two wonderful people who dedicated their time and talents to this project. First, thank you to Marty Yochum Casey for the cover design and your patience with us while we debated and changed our minds. Second, thank you to Dr. Fred Dobson for his time, energy and insightful questions. Your editing made this a much better book!

Table of Contents

Foreword

If you have the courage to love boldly and are willing to learn simple steps to enjoy
richer relationships, you'll be sizzling soon!

Fulfilling relationships are possible…with our lovers, with our children, with our friends and co-workers. From *Fizzle to Sizzle* offers you the premise that understanding relationships can be a way of reaching a deeper understanding of what makes each person tick! This awareness is your golden arrow to identify your needs and values and to be crystal clear about what you want in your relationships. Without the golden arrow, you are lost in the dark. Going blind and unarmed into relationships will cause you pain, discord, and unnecessary trauma.

From *Fizzle to Sizzle* explains why people act as they do, how to respond to them, and how to stay true to your own values. This book offers you knowledge of four crucial tools: the HUG method of accessing your truth, how your core temperaments influence you, how to make values-based choices, and how to repair emotional reactions that hijack you from your relationship.

Open your eyes and see relationships clearly.

Just as there is a science to human bonding after birth, there is a science to how humans bond and love through all the stages of life. Science explains the influence our genetic predispositions have on our ability to give love and receive love, and how we are likely to respond emotionally to others. This knowledge can be applied to understanding relationships with our life partners, parents and children, friends or colleagues.

Results you can expect:

• Fall in love all over again with yourself, your lover, your teen or your toddler.

• Find the partner of your dreams.

• Improve communication and connection in all of your relationships.

• Approach challenging times with integrity and resolve.

• Know how to repair any relationship at home or at work.

Relationships are practical, yet purposeful.

Whatever your relationship, the practical purpose is about sharing, learning, and managing together. Yet when relationships stretch you beyond your comfort zone, each one offers an opportunity to learn its higher purpose. Do you need to learn clearer communication, respect for others, forgiveness, or celebration of togetherness?

Together, the four crucial tools—core temperaments, values, emotional hijacking and HUG are your secrets to relationship repair. You will learn to:

- Recognize patterns that interfere with good relationships.

- Decode others' behaviors and discern which values drive their choices.

- Determine emotional predispositions and whether people respond or are reacting from emotional memories.

- Select and manage your communication temperament for maximum effect.

- Repair your relationships with lovers, kids, or coworkers.

- Help others make better choices for rich, loving, fulfilling relationships.

Introduction

Why You Need THIS Relationship Book

You are doing things day in and day out that drain energy out of your relationships, cost you peace of mind, cause you stress, and leave you feeling lonelier than you like. The juice is gone and motivation may have fizzled out of all of your relationships.

The worst part is that you aren't operating at your best, even though you may have the deepest desire to fix your relationship. How about starting over so you can infuse your relationship with inspiration and excellence? Would you like your relationship to sizzle?

Here's the truth. Keep doing what you're doing and you'll get the same fizzle. Albert Einstein defined insanity as doing the same thing over and over again and expecting different results. Are you ready to make the change? Are you willing to step into a new phase of your relationship and get significant, startling, even sizzling results?

If you want to start making those changes right now, commit to action. Surround yourself with people who will help you step up and stop old patterns. Hold this book to your heart and pledge yourself to creating a sizzling relationship. We are giving you a proven system to make it easy for you to start right now.

In fact, why not make that commitment right now?

I, _____, commit to repairing my relationships and moving from fizzle to sizzle using the four crucial tools.

_____

Signature   Date

What Does The Signature to Commitment Mean?

Commitment is a very important value that we'll mention often in this book. Without commitment, you cannot move forward because you are always looking back over your shoulder.

Aubrey was 30 years old and freshly divorced from a man who was physically abusive. Then she married Ross, who was 10 years older than she was. Neither of them questioned their instant connection. They knew they were soul mates! Their values seemed complementary. Aubrey felt safe with Ross, and he felt appreciated by her. She didn't care about his money, just his company. He felt he'd found a woman who was happy with herself and respected the alone time needed for his work as a public speaker and author.

In six months, their surprised friends and family gathered to celebrate their wedding and secretly hoped for their happiness. However wedding guests questioned Aubrey's motivation or wondered about mal-intent. They wondered how Ross would find time to have a partner when his life was already full.

What no one knew is that Aubrey asked for a two-year commitment from Ross, renewable every two years until she could feel safe within herself. This was her back door if she wanted out, and she asked Ross to agree ahead of time. Both of them entered the relationship with open eyes. This was a smart psychological move on her part, because now she could look forward, without her fear of being abused creeping into her psyche saying, "get out, get out now."

Ross and Aubrey made a commitment and fully expected to renew it after two years. Like Aubrey, all of us have relationship difficulties. Like Ross, all of us have in mind the kind of intimate or friend we would like to be with.

What you need to move forward like they did is commitment. Commitment says to our intimate partner, "I love you enough to stick it out with you. I am willing to learn to love and find different ways to create connection, not separation." Commitment allows us to make it through work transitions and accept or not the terms that employment offers. Commitment allows us to adapt to our children and not parent them in the negative way we were parented.

Your signature to commitment means that you make a pledge to do the following:

- Make an effort to repair your relationship, whether with your partner, your child, a friend or colleague.

- Take responsibility for your motivation and actions.

- Offer no excuses.

- Take the agreed-upon actions.

- If you make a mistake, then accept responsibility, apologize, and begin again.

Commitment is the real glue that gets you through transitions that negatively influence your relationships, such as the changes your children grow through, the economic garbage that lands on your doorstep, or the pressures that cause both of you to hide and wish the world away. These events do strengthen our resilience, but we have to be committed to keep moving forward and being focused.

Relationships without commitment don't grow and are like a loaf of bread without yeast: they don't rise and will inevitably fall under the pressure of everyone's expectations. It's hard to love another adult, child, or intimate partner with true love. True love is about respect, allowing the other person to be him or herself, and about honesty in all of your relationships. At times it's difficult for you to recognize, nourish and commit to your own self-love, growth, and personal development. Commit now to improving your relationship with your self and those in your life.

Putting the Sizzle into Your Relationships Starts Here

Have you ever had one of those ah-ha moments when the light dawned and revealed the solution to the mystery of relationships? Your understanding suddenly expanded! You might have wondered why you didn't see it before. Reading *From Fizzle to Sizzle* is that kind of eye-opening, spectacular experience that teaches you to use several simple, basic tools. The four crucial tools are key ingredients you need to make sure your relationships work. Rather than react, your new understanding of the four tools will help you respond and observe the issue with a new perspective. Here are the four tools that you'll be learning:

1. **Four Core Temperaments** – the genetic predisposition or tendency to learn and interact in certain ways. Understanding these four temperaments helps you to decipher behaviors.

2. **Core Values** – These are the beliefs you hold dear to your heart that guide your decisions. People rarely know their values consciously. If you make a decision that goes against what you solidly believe, you get anxious, scared, irritated with yourself, worry - all of these signal you with a strong message: you are out of alignment with yourself. *Your head is thinking about it, your heart doesn't feel truly committed to the decision, and your gut may be acting up.* Fizzle to Sizzle *will get you back on track.*

3. **Head-Heart-Gut™** – also called HUG – is an alignment process where you discern the feelings of or listen to the inner voices of your head, heart and gut. HUG is the signature work of Dr. Caron Goode and shows you how to access, trust, and use your inner wisdom to make your relationships the best, and be true to yourself in the process.

4. **Repairing Emotional Hijacking** – Your emotional tendencies are adaptable—that is, your cultural and familial interactions either strengthened your natural emotional resilience or stunted it. Either you learned to be independent or to ask for help. You learned to be a doormat or to stand up for yourself. You learned to worry or to trust. Whatever knee-jerk emotional reactions come up in your relationship, rest assured that each one is an emotional memory that happened at an earlier age. You will learn to recognize and change these in the relationship repair system.

You cannot give yourself away in relationships. You must bring your best to the relationship.

Tool One Is Core Temperament

The first tool for relationship repair is to identify your core temperament or temperaments. You are born with a core temperament. When you understand this tool, you'll be able to read people like a book. You will develop finesse in repairing or cultivating relationships when you decipher how people adapt over time. If you imagine your core temperament to be like the roots of a tree, you see that they take hold and spread out through rock, sand, dirt, and more; the species grows true to its form but is molded and shaped by nature's elements.

Core temperaments – From birth you are biologically predisposed to approach the world with a specific core temperament or core temperaments. You enter into a life-long process of adaptation to your environment, to your relations with caregivers, siblings, parents, or teachers, and, eventually, to the broader social environment.

- Your core temperament is your genetic tendency to interact in predictable patterns with people, data and information, or your environment.

- Your core temperament includes how you react emotionally, how you respond under stress, and how you learn best. Imagine how YOU could choose to communicate if you could predict how an intimate might respond?

- You could have one strong temperament or usually a combination of two or three. A few people even exhibit traits of all four core temperaments throughout their lives. These tendencies are present in infancy and continue to grow throughout childhood and adulthood. We have named these core temperaments for your fun and humor!

  - **Bulldozer** – competitive visionary who achieves, challenges, and learns best by doing.

- **Detective** – shy perfectionist who works with data, concepts, numbers, and learns best via seeing.
- **Border Collie** – empathic supporter, who likes appreciation, practices common sense and learns best through hearing.
- **Ringmaster** – influential communicator, who teaches, speaks, sells, writes and learns best through feeling and intuition.

In real life, your environment modifies and shapes your core predispositions through a combination of biological, experiential, interpersonal, chemical, and social factors. How you bond with others and how well you adapt to situations influences how you relate to people and your ability to be intimate later in life.

Can you see how this information can be pure gold? Imagine how your relationships will improve when you can anticipate and influence people's reactions in relationships. Once you understand your core temperament and learn how you related to people early on, you'll trace your emotional reactions and see who triggers those in you now and why.

Alan, the Detective temperament, loved his wife Ella dearly, but when she spoke in a whiny voice he had to leave the room. Ella, the supportive Border Collie, thought he was angry and withdrew from her for some reason she couldn't decipher. Ella also withdrew and felt unappreciated. Always looking for clues, Alan kept asking himself why he walked away from his wife so abruptly. When they finally talked it through, Alan confessed that her whiny voice sounded like his mom, and then Ella remembered her mother always withdrawing when she was angry. What a relief! They were reacting from emotional memories: their reactions had absolutely nothing to do with their present situation.

Like Alan and Ella, you'll have clues to your partner's emotions and will learn how to respond and defuse situations or say the right words so you can be heard. Your emotions affect how you ***see and interpret*** the world. They can also affect how you ***react or behave.*** For example, if you feel listless, you find it difficult to take action. If you are feeling angry or not well you are prone to say and do hurtful things. If you are feeling love or happiness you want to share those feelings and will act in support of others. Your emotional predispositions tend to influence your behaviors, and most of your reactions are memories from past situations. You must break these emotional habits for relationships to progress, otherwise, you stay stuck at age 3, 6, 8, or 15.

The Second Tool is Values - Values Are the Guiding Light of Relationships

Values drive the best—as well as the poorest—choices you make. The second tool to relationship repair is defining the personal values that you believe are the guiding lights in your life. When you are not clear about why you act as you do, or your gut reacts when you make a decision, then you are not clear about your values. *From Fizzle to Sizzle* will help you to know and prioritize your values for a strong inner foundation.

For example, we often hear conflicting statements from parents, even when both phrases are based on the same value of loving one's children. James and Sara said, "We are staying together despite our arguments and disagreements for the sake of the kids." Chris and Pat said, "We are divorcing because we love our kids and can't put them through our disagreements and arguments for the rest of their childhoods." Values drive the choices you eventually defend in relationships. Even if circumstances change, your values about loving your children remain the same.

You may have a mentor whose values you align with and this steers your career choices. A friend may have been spanked as a child and now highly values nurturing children. He or she may want to have a large family, and as a prospective partner, you need to know this.

Maybe you respect your partner in relationship and want to please him or her: you cave and say yes to a disagreeable situation. When you give up your values or strong beliefs to another person, organization, or corporation, your gut twinges. You worry: the decision just doesn't sit well with you. These signals tell you that your values are compromised. Here are other examples of compromised values:

The educational supervisor in Caron's school district suggested she ask her Master's Thesis advisor for an approval six months ahead of the deadline, so she could graduate and be promoted within the district. Caron's gut twinged; she sweated and got cotton-mouthed when she asked her advisor for the personal favor. At age 22 and new to the school district, Caron assumed that her supervisor knew her advisor, or knew that skipping the approval procedure was appropriate for the new school funded position. Neither assumption was true. Her academic advisor said no, and Caron lost credibility and respect by trying to cut corners.

Marty's high school friends described her as "wholesome." Marty rarely partied with her friends, but the senior prom was an exceptional opportunity to have some fun before heading off to her Ivy League university for summer school. Several friends tried to get Marty drunk, teasing her about being a "holier-than-thou bitch." Marty finally chose to leave the escalating private party when a friend from French class offered her a soda. Marty's intuitive signals rang loud and clear that this acquaintance spiked the drink. She always followed her intuition and saved herself a lot of embarrassing moments. Sticking to her personal beliefs made her strong and gave her courage to trust her own common sense.

In *From Fizzle to Sizzle,* you'll clarify your values and learn how they can improve your relationships as well as your confidence and courage. Do you remember how good confidence feels - how high you hold your head when feeling courageous? You can have these wonderful feelings every day when you are aligned with your truth: calm in your gut, happy in your heart, and assured in your mind.

We share how to stay aligned with your values and beliefs in relationships through the third tool, called Head-Heart-Gut.™

The Third Tool is Head-Heart-Gut™ = HUG

The Head-Heart-Gut™ (we call it HUG) method for staying aligned within yourself and also in relationships is the signature work of Dr. Caron Goode. Her method specifically evolved from 1988 through 2003 in her therapeutic work with families, educational work with children, and transpersonal-spiritual work with women with health issues.

People come to counselors and psychotherapists to find answers to issues, and Dr. Goode taught people of all ages to access their own answers. After finding their answers, most people did not trust what they knew to be true or were fearful of making mistakes and doing the wrong thing based on limited beliefs and past traumas. By practicing HUG, people gained confidence, felt self-assured and made better, more successful decisions. With the advent of the life-coaching field, the HUG method became popular for coaching others to walk their talk by listening, journaling, and practicing. The method instills confidence in accessing your inner knowing, paired with common sense and logic.

The Fourth Tool Is Managing Emotional Hijacking

Emotional hijacking means that fearful, traumatic, or stressful patterns of your childhood pop up when triggered in your life as an adult. When you are having a normal conversation, hijacking elicits the stress response pattern of your temperament: get angry, withdraw and worry, laugh it off and escape; feel abandoned or made fun of. As an adult you are flooded with fears or anxieties that are really only emotional memories. The good news is that once you name them, you can tame them. We show you precisely how to do this.

Together, these four crucial tools—core temperaments, values, HUG and managing emotional hijacking are your secrets to relationship repair. In the next steps you will learn to

- Recognize patterns that interfere with good relationships.

- Decode others' behaviors—discern which values drive their choices.

- Determine emotional predispositions and whether people respond to or are reacting from emotional memories.

- Select and manage your communication temperament for maximum effect.

- Repair your relationships with partners, kids, or coworkers.

- Help others make better choices for rich, loving, fulfilling relationships.

From this important knowledge you will learn how to influence others, communicate clearly, and appreciate them for the gifts you couldn't see before. To accomplish this, we first present an overview of the steps of relationship repair; in subsequent chapters you will complete each of these steps.

Overview - How to Use the Four Crucial Tools

Here is your overview of how to use the four crucial Tools. Take note of the steps and what is required to successfully complete each one. In this section, you'll see why relationships can fall apart and what makes them work. The steps necessary to repair old emotional patterns alert you to be aware of your problems and another's issues as you read the next section.

Assess

The first step is your self-assessment for personal awareness; you will use this as a barometer to gauge the temperament of your relationships. When you understand a factor that drives your reactions, you can name and tame it, change it, and feel completely at peace with yourself. For example, your core temperament reaction of not feeling appreciated and getting depressed wearies you and your children - or your core drive to achieve beyond all else tells others in your relationships that you do not value them. If you can name it, then you can tame it.

1. Identify your core temperament and use it to define and understand your natural inclination when reacting to people, whether intimates or coworkers, as well as to understand your reactions to stress, tasks and the environment around you. See Section II.

2. Discover where those tendencies come from – your childhood environment or current stressful circumstances. Most reactions are simply **emotional memories** from events that happened as you grew up and they have become ingrained within you. We call these learned responses. When you jump to judgment, are nice because you can't say no, or brush off a friend rudely, you are reacting spontaneously as your emotional memories surface. We provide questions to guide you in assessing and understanding these tendencies in Section V.

Clarify

3. Identify and clarify the values you feel most strongly about; you might get defensive about them in a relationship. We provide you with questions to guide you through this exercise in Section III.

4. Complete the relationship profile charts throughout the book and be clear on what you bring to the table as a parent, partner, or professional.

5. An intimate partner also brings a profile, and your conversations about relationship repair must also take into account your partners values and temperaments. Ask your partner to complete steps one through four. Compare temperaments and values and you will begin to see patterns emerge and instant possibilities for relationship repair that will take you from fizzle to sizzle. Even with teams in a business setting, having each individual complete steps one through four and then as a group comparing temperaments and values can lead to a more productive and fulfilling work environment.

Review

6. Review your formative years and see whether you met the developmental milestones for relationships that all humans pass through. You'll remember your development in handling relationships for each decade and add this to your relationship profile.

Based upon your profile, be aware the next time you have an emotional flare-up. Chart your emotions on a calendar or in a journal. Note which incident or emotion sparked the flare-up. Just start naming them and taming them, one at a time.

Repair Using HUG

7. At this point, you know your core temperament(s). You are aware of potentially reactionary memories that might flare up in your life as a professional, a parent, a partner or a friend. Just like any favorite recipe, relationships get better every time you choose repair and connection. What would you like to repair? List your goals, write down questions about them, and then go get a hug from HUG.

The questions you take to HUG are straightforward and written clearly. There is no room in your questions for maybe, could, should, what if, and such. Questions that derive clear answers are to be found by looking at benefits, best action right now, appropriate actions going forward, best timing, most effective results, clarity, the higher good of all, and what benefits all: the focus is on moving forward with a congruent response from HUG.

8. You make new choices by knowing what you want. Asking HUG questions, considering the internal answers, and choosing an option to try becomes the model for relationship repair and connec-

tion. The HUG chapter walks you through specific steps and examples.

We guarantee that by the end of this book, you will be able to implement these steps, using our four crucial tools to repair any relationship. We want to remind you of two things as you begin to move your relationships from fizzle to sizzle:

1. It only takes one person to be the change agent in a relationship. You can be the change you want to see by practicing and implementing each of the four tools and staying committed to creating a sizzling relationship.

2. These tools take practice. Successful relationships stem from your willingness to commit to the ongoing process of relationship repair. Remember your signature pledging 100% commitment.

Chapter One

Why are Relationships so Hard?

When interacting with other people, it would be much wiser to observe and learn rather than to judge and condemn. ~The Daily Guru

The steps of relationship repair are easy to follow once you know how to identify potential crises before they escalate into national disasters. Most of you find yourself in a crisis before realizing how you got there.

- How many times has a child said to a parent, "You hurt me." - yet the parent did not raise her hand or his voice. What emotional atmosphere did the child pick up on and express?
- A co-worker seethes quietly for only so long before needing to blow off steam, and you are in the vicinity. You may or may not choose to respond if it means losing work time or getting sucked into a rescue.
- Anger rises in your partner quickly - like a volcano spewing fire and ash. You don't like being caught in the aftermath: you can see it coming and help your partner to control such angry responses.
- Your friend complains all through your scheduled date for Sunday brunch. When you get home, you are tired, wondering why. Did you realize the friend drained you?

Before you start asking questions and attempting to repair issues, let us share with you some of the causes behind the symptoms you want to change. Knowing the cause may change the way you ask the questions. All relationships have stressors, problems, or frustrations. You have to name them when you see them, and then tame them. Relationship discord comes from one of three sources:

1. Clashing core temperaments
2. Conflicting values
3. Emotional memories

One example of clashing core temperaments involves Reon and Maggie. Maggie, age 25, attends college and is completing courses for nursing certification. She has a "thinker" temperament, just like a

Detective who loves to learn, study, and apply her knowledge, especially during the time Reon is deployed. Now that he is back home, she is still adjusting to him being around.

Reon joined the Marines right after high school and has thrived because he loves a good challenge. The difficult does not daunt him; he moves forward like a Bulldozer with his plans to run a marathon. Now that he is no longer a Marine, he wants to keep up the pace and physical conditioning.

Reon is a doer; a Bulldozer. He wants to run, and he does: easy as that! He wants Maggie to join him for a run at 4 am.

"Hey, sleepyhead, get up. Let's go out," he slaps her on the butt, waking her out of a deep sleep.

"What the f---?" She rolls over and covers her head.

"Come on. I told you I was going for an early run. Come on."

Sitting up in disgust and throwing the pillow at Reon, Maggie screeches at him for the second time, "What the crap! You said you were going. Then go. I've got to be up for classes in 2 hours, so leave me alone!"

"You and your books, Megs! You need to get out and DO stuff, girl!" Reon laughs as he remembers his wife isn't at her best in the morning. He knows he will hear about this later.

Reon the Bulldozer's high energy and activity level clash with quiet, analytical Maggie the Detective, who will take a book over sweaty running any day. The incident isn't a big one, and they'll live through it, but it does demonstrate how not understanding each other's core temperament leads to disrespect and disconnection.

Most intimate partnerships face similar issues...money, sex, and other arguments stoke the fires of discontent between couples.

Our thoughts run rampant with angry words. We don't communicate our real feelings: *"I don't trust him; she nags; he's a hypochondriac!"* We blame each other for discord, disagreements, and misunderstandings.

Parenting issues are 98% miscommunication errors caused by stress and by parent and child being unaware of each other's core temperaments.

Jillian has little empathy for her son: she is a good example of the Bulldozer type. She is a high-powered mom attorney accustomed to managing her team of paralegals in a thriving law practice. She is up at 5 am and ready to get out the door by 6 am, if it weren't for her distracted, dawdling son. She has little patience for him because she does not understand he is like a Ringmaster watching the intricate circus in his mind. He daydreams and sings songs in his head. He is blank about time, even for a 9-year-old who knows his schedule. If she took the time to learn how to communicate with him, she would enjoy "doing" a lot of creative activities together and creating a morning routine that works for both of them.

A Huge Truth!

The discontent of a partner, parent or friend with a different core temperament is never about the topic or event: the discontent is *always* about someone's feelings or emotions. Our uncensored emotional rants only hinder our relationships.

Get ready to change all that.

The solution is to have in place systems or routines for diffusing clashes and emotional outbursts, which are really emotional memories rearing their ugly smirks. Through the relationship repair steps you will personalize the system of responses for your relationships.

Here is how repair works:

1. After learning your temperament and your partner's temperament, you determine where you clash and if you are compatible. Then start using HUG to create solutions, compromises, and appropriate actions.

2. If you clash, then you learn to temperament-shift to your partner's temperament. You communicate in a way your partner can hear you. If her Border Collie temperament needs appreciation, learn how easy it is to say, "I appreciate what you do." If the Bulldozer golfer is rushing out the door, see how easy it is to say, "Stop long enough so I can wish you a good game and say goodbye." Or perhaps more honestly, "I am thrilled you are going on this golf tour. I love my alone time for writing. Have fun."

3. You consider the partner's values and weigh their importance in the matter. For example, he is a chef who desires the most expensive kitchen gear for his enjoyment of cooking healthy food for his family. She doesn't mind cooking, but neither does she clean up after herself. Values clash when she burns a pan, when he demands she clean up, and dinner is a silent affair. Learn to clarify values and show respect for the common areas of the house or co-ownership of things around the house.

4. You review your emotional patterns and see how your reactions are residues from your past. We call emotional memories that take you over before you can stop them **emotional hijacking**. Your

survival patterns kick in when you feel threatened and old emotions start playing like your favorite broken record. We'll show you how to name them and tame them.

The four crucial tools provided in this book are your guides. They focus on YOU first. You'll find your own values, your core temperaments, learn to check in with yourself for guidance, and learn about your own response patterns in tough situations.

You'll learn to ask, "Is this working or not?" If not, you change your nonworking reactions into responsiveness. Relationship repair requires only one person like you, dedicated and desirous of seeing better result to create significant change.

What Supports Relationship Renewal and Repair?

Relationship repair and renewal is not only possible - it is the natural result of loving your way through a problem. Yet it requires the commitment to love a partner enough to speak up, to love a child enough to model better behaviors, to care professionally about your work environment so you take positive action.

You have to be willing to

- Watch for those moments when conversation about change can happen.
- Be ready to invite your partner into that conversation because you share a common goal for a better relationship.
- Overcome your fear of challenging conversations by focusing on the best possible outcome and speaking from your heart.
- Notice a child's growing agitation before it escalates into irritability and tears, and be responsive to the in-the-moment feelings.

Living with a child or partner or working every day with disagreeable people takes patience. Sometimes we are too tired to face discord or manage meaningful conversations. Most of us don't speak up and are afraid to hurt another's feelings, especially if we live with them. We push words down or hold feelings inside until we erupt harshly in anger. We covertly sabotage the relationship in a desperate attempt to get the other person's attention. Aren't you ready for something dramatically different?

Think how relaxed you would feel being able to speak up. You feel an incredible freedom as you watch for the opportunities to grow and expand communication. Always be mindful that you are a change agent. To repair relationships is a matter of you being willing, ready, and committed to positive action. Make sure you have signed the Signature to Commitment on page 2 before continuing.

Ending Relationship Ignorance Now

Being able to interpret someone's core temperament and what he or she values coupled with listening to your inner guru is going to make you change the way you see and think about people. For example, for years the public perception of people who were obese or overweight was that they were out-of-control eaters with emotional issues. That perception was based on ignorance, and is equivalent to judging other people.

What we now know is that the body's ability to metabolize food and fat is a system of complex hormonal interactions, and one disturbance in one hormone starts a cascade of hormonal miscues in metabolizing and handling fat stores. Other influences - like what a mother eats during pregnancy and the genetic influence from our grandparents' generations - can cause the body to store fats. We now know that certain substances in our food chain add unwanted and excess poundage—even when they have the name "diet" in them.

With new knowledge, you'll end relationship ignorance. You'll find your personal "Ah-ha!" in discovering how to see another's core temperament. You'll finally understand the common language of valuing your relationships.

Relationship Repair Basics

The type of human being we prefer reveals the contours of our heart.
~Jose Ortega y Gasset

There are healthy ways to overcome relationship issues if love and mutual respect are the foundations that support your interactions. In a parent-child relationship love is usually a given, whereas a relationship with a co-worker may merely be friendly. The culture of a business organization may dictate whether you can build a caring or respectful relationship with co-workers. In a work environment, it is human nature that you deal with to gain respect. You will find the four crucial tools of temperament, values, repairing emotional hijackings and HUG™ are your most valuable tools for repairing any relationship.

In a personal partnership, while one partner alone can make a dynamic difference, relationship repair works best if both partners are willing to approach it together using a system that makes them aware of their own patterns and the patterns in their relationship.

Relationship repair helps you explore and explain dynamics such as
- Do your core temperaments clash?

- Are your core temperaments compatible?
- Are your reactions in relationship a conflict of values?
- Are the choices you are defending substantiated in reality or based in the past?
- If it feels like a pattern from the past, then name it and tame it through conversation.
- Move through commitment to action.

Leave the challenges in the next room until you find deeper insight through the suggestions in this book. A mutual commitment to being clear and compassionate moves you forward.

Here is a reminder of what you committed to with your signature at the beginning of this book:

- ***I agree to put a system for relationship repair in place and fix communication problems as they surface.***

- ***I make a commitment to take time for conversation and compassion.***

- ***I am ready!***

Are the Issues Always The Same?

Yes: for the majority of people the issues come up over and over because each person in a relationship has habitual reactions. Over time, you learn to avoid hot topics. You become accustomed to pushing each other's buttons. Even children in their early years sense what makes a parent tense, relaxed, angry, or withdrawn, and they react to their parents' emotional patterns. At work, you might avoid an issue and withdraw rather than confront, be assertive or communicate. Let's review the basic ways in which people of different core temperaments clash:

1. **Issues of stress:** When the world spits, squeezes, and slams into your life, you need to feel safe. Based upon your core temperament, you might

- Withdraw and view the world from a distance.
- Endure until a crash-and-burn cycle kicks in.
- Take it in stride and adapt.
- Hold it in and become sick.
- Escape to another physical place or escape into the mind for a dream respite.

Stress can be managed through fun, party, rest, and rejuvenation. Managing stress works in relationships. The coping mechanisms mentioned above are okay once in a while, but become chronic problems if you let them become habits.

2. **Issues of time:** We don't often encounter people who are able to go with the flow these days. The perception is that time drags or that time is speeding up. In relationship, time issues appear when

- You have no concept of time and move to a different internal rhythm.
- You have no regard for time, and your partner views this as disrespectful.

- You are a watcher of time both for yourself and for others: as their self-appointed time-keeper you drive them nuts.
- You live in the past and continually drag it into the present.
- You dream about the future and make big plans but never bother to implement them.

The best way to manage time when other people are involved is to be present with them and have mutual goals and a plan to integrate your values as a means of problem solving.

3. **Issues of dependence versus independence:** The balance is tricky. You can feel smothered if a partner's needs become neediness; you want to back away and have some independence so you can breathe. On the other hand, too much independence can breed loneliness and withdrawal.

4. **Issues of empathy:** You demonstrate behavior patterns that show a lack of empathy for others which broadcasts *I am insensitive.* On the other hand, empathy can be overdone:

- You care for another too much.
- You want to help too much.
- You absorb another's pain - and then blame him or her for it.
- You can be so self-centered that you want to be - may even need to be the center of attention (this is normal, not narcissistic, for younger kids.) Moreover, you may feel entitled to that attention.

5. **Issues ranging from being self-centered to narcissistic**: Let's pause for a word about entitlement, which loosely means in our society that a person feels they deserve something and have a right to it, "just because I do." They don't earn it or pay their dues, so to speak. This sense of entitlement is presently a huge issue in Western cultures. In psychological parlance, other names for entitlement syndrome are self-centeredness or selfishness, leading to narcissism.

- "Self-centered" means thinking or referring only to one's self. All children and teens pass through this stage where each one is the center of his or her world, and through the development of empathy, learning about other people's feelings and situations, they outgrow self-centeredness. If a person does not outgrow it, then parents recognize it in their children and partners observe it in their spouses as selfishness.
- Selfishness is looking out for "number one." Other traits of selfishness include greed, grandiose thinking, insensitivity to others, making self more important than other, and having unreasonable expectations.
- From our perspective, "Entitlement" includes the perception that one deserves regard, power, attention, and more. The traits impinge eventually on all people in relationship. Behaviors of entitlement include being demanding, aggressive, confrontational, controlling, righteous, argumentative, intrusive, and even abusive. There is no room for empathy.

- Narcissism is a condition of disordered thinking, and needs the help of a mental health professional. Such disordered thinking resembles a state of continual grandiosity: an overwhelming need for admiration, and complete lack of empathy. Like a queen in bygone days, others are to be used and abused. In today's world, few of us tolerate the king\queen syndrome in modern relationships.

6. **Temperament clashes:** The concept that people's energies clash is really the perception that one core temperament does not get along with or lacks understanding of another. Clients often ask why people are attracted to each other. Do opposites attract - or is it just biochemistry of survival? Are we really reacting to mommy and daddy? The answer from research is that we favor and attract to us people like ourselves, especially people with the same emotional patterns and cut from the same cultural cloth. We'll discuss in more detail in a later chapter how temperament clashes result from a lack of understanding of partner interaction patterns - especially when the patterns stem from core survival demands.

Back to Entitlement in Relationships

Some people, who have suffered as children, may feel their parents should give them money, or help support them because of their pain. Such demanding individuals are often referred to as emotional vampires who prey on kind people. This behavior pattern, if continued with no effort at changing it, can lead to narcissism. On the other hand, innocence and naiveté are sometimes confused with entitlement.

Lewis, a 50-ish Dad who adored and protected his three daughters always reassured them by telling them that they were beautiful and would marry loving men who would take care of them as he took care of them because he loved them. In his case, his daughters heard his message loud and clear. After college, the two eldest returned to live with their parents because they could not find "suitable" employment. Moreover, their adventuresome personalities led them to travel before settling down. In their youthful exuberance, they believed their dad would continue to support their life temperament rent-free and pay for their global travels. Unfortunately for Lewis, he didn't make it clear that they should be independent adults who paid their own way after they graduated from college. The daughters' sense of entitlement was fostered by Lewis' parenting, as is most children's sense of what they are entitled to. Research shows that children's entitlement comes from permissive parenting: that is parenting with few boundaries or expectations.

Chapter Two

The First Tool: Core Temperaments

In this assessment you become self-aware, first by identifying your core temperament(s), and then by responding to the questions or statements that best describe your most consistent attitudes and behaviors.

You'll determine whether you are one core temperament or a combination of the following:

- Bulldozer
- Border Collie
- Detective
- Ringmaster

You'll determine how…

- You respond to stress
- You learn and think best
- You may be predisposed to emotionally respond in relationships

You'll discover whether you prefer…

- Being with people
- Dealing with data and numbers
- Pushing your limits
- Being a creative entrepreneur

> ***The future*** *has several names. For the weak, it is the impossible. For the fainthearted, it is the unknown. For the thoughtful and valiant, it is the ideal. ~Victor Hugo*

Introduction

As adults, we notice that the people in our lives have diverse approaches to handling stress, tackling tasks, and navigating through life's sticky situations. Parents are aware how differently their children act out, respond to people, and explore their environment. Some kids leap into life and others tiptoe. We're all born with a natural predisposition to interact with people and do tasks in a certain way, and it's this unique constellation of how we do what we do that is our own core temperament.

In addition to being part of the force that drives us to *do what we do, the way we do it*, our core temperament is the foundation from which we

- Build our values.
- Shape our relationship preferences.
- Formulate our reactions to the world around us.

Core temperaments are why some people thrive when working on deadline and others can barely function by the clock. It's why some kids learn by reading and others by doing. We are briefly reviewing these four temperaments first so you can start to think about the language and pick out some of your own characteristics. In the assessment section, we'll delve into the values, stress responses, time preferences, and learning preferences for each temperament. You'll be amazed when you see yourself!

Four Basic Core Temperaments

There are four distinct categories of core temperaments. These categories include the basic names, but for the sake of humor, we've added and will use throughout this book the following terms in bold. They are more fun and offer examples from everyday life by which you can remember the temperament traits. Read these stories first, and then assess your own temperament(s) with our Core Temperament Inventory.

1. The doer = the **Bulldozer**
2. The thinker = the **Detective**
3. The harmonizer = the **Border Collie**
4. The influencer = the **Ringmaster**

While there are bits and pieces of each personal temperament in all of us (and all of our children), you'll typically exhibit one to two dominant temperaments that influence the way you interact with your environment. Throughout your life span, you might rotate through all the core temperaments as you adapt to your environment.

Imagine a pool party on a hot summer day to which you've been invited to cool off.

- A **Bulldozer** type dives in and calls on the way into the water, "Last one in is a loser. I'll race you to the other side!" Doesn't he just love the challenge and thrives on competition?

- A **Detective** type finds a quieter place to dip her foot in to check the water temperature before venturing in. Shy of the noise and splashing, this observer watches and learns about the people around her before introducing herself and joining in.
- A **Border Collie** type might serve the drinks and snacks around the pool, or get in the water to play a game of tag or Marco Polo, while carefully ensuring that everyone's okay and playing nicely.
- The **Ringmaster** also jumps in the water and yells, "Watch my cannonball." He does love to make a big splash, making sure he is seen. He then organizes everyone into a game of water volleyball.

Each of the core temperaments approaches situations differently. Depending upon how you respond to the changing environments, you may need to adopt a different temperament. A few examples include:

- A **Bulldozer** who fell from a rock ledge and broke his leg while mountain climbing won't be doing that for a while. He might temporarily choose to become a Detective, reading, researching and making plans to climb the next mountain.
- A **Border Collie** may get sick too often because she is volunteering too much and isn't resting and rejuvenating herself. Her body has said enough, so her healing time might be spent at weekly spa appointments or a vacation at her favorite beach. She has learned so much about good health from her change that her creativity awakens the Ringmaster within her. She writes a book about what she has learned and enters the speaker's circuit to share her knowledge.

The Bulldozer

The Bulldozer is a high-achieving doer who gets tasks done and doesn't let anyone stand in his way. He loves adventure and rises to the challenge of moving a mountain or running a marathon. She likes being in charge and responsible for the team. Bringing strength of vision and a command of most situations, Bulldozers are leaders, visionaries, pushers, adrenaline junkies, and powerful competitors.

One top-notch Bulldozer named Tina agreed to share how her do-it attitude and Bulldozer temperament has shaped her life.

As a little girl, I was raised by two southern women on opposite sides of the temperament spectrum. My grandmother was tough as nails. By contrast, my sensitive mother was demure and agreeable. My grandmother earned labels like "bitchy," my mother was the nice one. I wanted to be anything BUT what my grandmother stood for, and worked hard to be more like my mother. I decided I would be nice and reserved in an acceptable way.

I had already earned my own B label in school – bossy – and even though I really wanted to be the 'nice' girl, there was an uncontrollable force within me that led me to speak up for injustices and to say what others didn't have the courage to say. I acted more like my grandmother than I ever anticipated. Still, I thought this was unacceptable and worked even harder to dial back the bossiness.

By the time I was 32 my bulldozer was virtually non-existent. I spent the first three years of my marriage trying to get someone else to tell my husband something for me. I needed alone time to reflect and ponder things, and he didn't seem to have that need. He wanted to be with me all the time! I signed us up for a counseling appointment so the counselor could help me tell him what I needed. This backfired when she told me I was asking too much. Bam! That fiery doer side of me engaged.

I began to be okay with the fiery part of me coming out, but found I couldn't let it come out until I had exhausted every other avenue. When the fiery part came out, it was usually in an unloving, blistering tone. This didn't feel good and certainly didn't feel like the "me" I wanted to be.

When my husband and I did the core temperament profiling, I realized in an instant that his Doer-Bulldozer is always attached to getting something accomplished. He is a man on a mission, and I'm the benefactor of that behavior - from getting us packed for vacations to ensuring every bit of technology runs well in our business. It isn't personal – he's just moving from start to finish.

I realized my own Bulldozer had been banished to the closet labeled 'things that are unacceptable." I had been suppressing this very important part of myself, and came to realize that it should be working for us just as my husband's temperament was.

Slowly but surely, I began to trust and value my Bulldozer side. I found it allowed me to be direct and to express myself honestly. My husband appreciated my directness in simply saying what I wanted; I also noticed that I had fewer eruptions, which meant less guilt. Perhaps the greatest gift is that our conversations have shifted away from avoiding issues and have been replaced with deep, thoughtful conversations. This has helped us to face our fears, envision the life we truly want and work together to create it."

Note that Bulldozer Tina married a person of similar core temperament. Her emotional pattern of trying to be nice and not speak directly emulated her mother, and this emotional response of the past did not work on her behalf, especially with her grandmother-type husband. She did not experience the intimacy or the sense of being valued that she desired in her relationship.

As a child Tina adapted well to her environment - and yet the maturing adult trying to emulate mom formed ineffective communication patterns. Tina's actions as an adult provide an excellent example for us all. She recognized a pattern from her past. She sought a counselor for help; she and her husband committed to working through their patterns; she was willing to let her authentic self step forth and learn to trust the world again as the child-self never could. Kudos to Tina for having the critical conversations with her husband and creating the life they desire together.

The Detective

The Detective loves data, ideas, numbers, and greatly respects order and structure. Think of the Detective as a perfectionist who likes to explain what is and envisions what could be. She worries about life a lot, and often researches solutions and designs answers to the problem that worries her. Sensitive by nature, the Detective does not take criticism too well although he can be a top team member who contributes overall. People value the Detective's expertise and problem-solving skills because she is logical, gives instruction, and values quality. Detectives enjoy stimulating discussion and sharing with a team. Read the story below for an example of how being a Detective impacted Martin's life as an adult.

Martin considered himself a lucky man when, thanks to his smart investments and aggressive savings, he retired from his work as an investment banker at a young age. The recent downturn in the economy has worried him since he lost quite a bit of money in the stock market. His concern is having enough money to support him and his wife for the rest of their lives. At 57 he is a young man. Martin realized that he needs to bring in some income, but is nervous about returning to work. He has not worked in over 10 years and the investment world has changed dramatically in that time.

Martin is insecure about his ability to catch up to the current times and new technology. He is intelligent but he is also a perfectionist who needs to get the job done right the first time. He has decided to start a bookkeeping business but drags his feet learning the new software and reaching out to potential clients. He insists on reading the information several times until he feels secure in the basic knowl-

edge.

Martin has lots of friends and contacts in his community and is an active volunteer with local charitable organizations. He is a great team player and community members often invite him to participate on committees or to organize fund raising events. Martin is meticulous with his record keeping and cautious with his own finances and those of the organizations he works with. People find Martin loyal and trustworthy and often turn to him for financial advice.

The Border Collie

The Border Collie is a supportive, interactive person who has empathy for others' feelings and the drive to help and support others. A Border Collie often plays the peacekeeper role in relationships, feeling anger at injustice and depression if his heart cup is not filled daily. The Border Collie values harmony and can be stubborn and depressed when things are not going her way. People with this temperament bring common sense to situations, like harmony in teamwork, and are steadfast, loyal and dependable. People with other personal temperaments depend on these nurturers and are nurtured by them.

While the Bulldozer is an action-oriented doer, the Border Collie is a heart-centered person whose pleasure is in helping and supporting others. Yet a Border Collie has her challenges. She can take too many things to heart. Concerns can weigh heavily on his shoulders. Her desire to see people happy and his desire to take care of his relationships, especially family members, are always in the forefront of his thoughts. When Border Collie people become quiet and withdrawn, be aware that they need appreciation: they need to get up and be involved in life again. Tricia shares how her temperament was shaped in her childhood and teen years.

Tricia's dad was a business executive who started his martinis at lunch and usually came home after work in a giddy, sleepy mood. He was a funny drunk who could make Tricia laugh. On the other hand, when angered, his booming voice made his auditory-sensitive child quake. After the terror of her early years, she avoided her father and identified more with her mother. Tricia's mother rushed the children home from school, through their piano and horn practices, and shooed them outside to play so the house was quiet when Daddy came home. Tricia always helped her mother with dinner so it was served promptly at 6 pm after the local news and before the evening television programs her dad liked to watch.

Rather than go outside and play with her brothers, Tricia helped her mom with housework, iron-

ing, cooking, and washing the dishes. She was a loyal Collie. She learned to sew, and as she grew older took over other chores for her mother, as was expected in her role as the only daughter. Internally, Tricia felt sorry for her mother and felt she deserved more respect. Tricia saw her mother as a dignified person who didn't just give money to Catholic charities, but also volunteered to help at hospice and church-related activities. She felt her father did not appreciate her mother, and once in a while heard her mother mutter negative things about her dad.

In her teen years Tricia was out of the house and active teaching Sunday school, teaching summer school as an assistant teacher, meeting with debate teammates, and travelling to debate tournaments. Yet she always befriended the bullied students and tutored those who slipped behind in language classes. Her need to help another seemed to go too far, and one good friend in high school told her she was meddling and to keep her nose out of her business. This incident was a wake-up call for Tricia who had assumed all people wanted help. She was wrong.

In college, she vowed to focus on her studies and earned her doctorate in clinical psychology. Her early work in a psychiatric hospital seemed to make her chronically ill, as if she wore the burdens of her clients. Her own supervisor called her condition empathy fatigue *and suggested she become a teaching professor, and not work directly with clients unless she could develop better boundaries and emotional resilience. She did become a professor and spent her years teaching and delegated her "helping" to her favorite charities. Occasionally she experienced depression, which she focused into volunteer hospice work. That seemed to feed her soul and gave her a reason for living.*

The Ringmaster

T**he Ringmaster** flourishes in friendships that laud their creativity and entrepreneurship. They value their freedom above all else. They love to indulge their senses and seek pleasure. Because of their persuasiveness and charisma they often become artists, authors, actors, speakers. They are the movers and shakers of the world who love expressing their opinions and influencing others. The Ringmaster is comfortable as the center of attention and loves to create and play with good friends.

Suzy is a creative mom of twin boys, aged 8. She is active in influencing her children's education by reading to children in the twins' classroom and teaching art projects one afternoon a week as part of the after-school program. She runs a scrapbooking business and loves getting other moms together to share the latest techniques, gadgets, and her newest creations with them. She is a great sales person and makes

good money working part-time selling advertising for the area's local parenting magazine.

Suzy loves where she is in her life right now, but it wasn't always that way. She started smoking pot in college, mostly out of curiosity and to be with the in crowd of artists on campus. Her excellent grades and outstanding design portfolio landed her a great job at a boutique, high-end, advertising company after graduation. The more she smoked - the more creative she felt and the less traditional the ad campaigns became. The company loved her and she found herself thinking she could do no wrong.

She was invited to join the company's "lunch group" which met Fridays for martini lunches and extended their business meetings well into the afternoon. But Suzy was uncomfortable with the amount of alcohol consumed, and she knew she did not hold her liquor well. But this was office politics and she was determined to succeed. She did succeed in becoming addicted to alcohol. Ironically, she was fired because the addiction interfered with her work production and resulted in a loss of sales.

As a recovering alcoholic, Suzy puts her family first. In any group setting she is still the life of the party and is a creative woman- but at home Suzy struggles with staying organized, keeping the kids in a regular routine and getting things done on time. She laughs about her disheveled home and rarely takes herself too seriously.

Her husband is a financial planner who prefers his home to be well-organized and pays close attention to the family finances. Suzy rarely manages to hold on to receipts and sometimes forgets to pay the bills on time. She loves her home to be full of laughter and spends a great deal of time playing with her children, helping them with homework and redecorating the house.

She and her husband struggle to find a balance between his need for quiet time and her need to be with people and to be on the move. She has learned to schedule play dates with friends or take the odd art class at the local community college in order to get time away from home and kids and to fuel her creative spirit.

As a mom, Suzy is warm, loving, and fun to be with, but she struggles with routines, helping the kids get projects turned in on time, or remembering to return that pesky permission slip! Her husband has long understood that Suzy will never be the housekeeper he imagined her to be. Although he had hopes of changing her core temperament, he finally hired a housekeeper.

Are you beginning to identify your core temperament? You may already recognize yourself from reading the descriptions of the core temperaments presented in this section. Take a few moments now to complete the Core Temperaments Brief Inventory on pages 27 to 30 to confirm what your dominant and secondary core temperaments are.

Core Temperaments: A Brief Inventory

Instructions: Please read the sentence in the left column, determine whether or not the sentence sounds like how you act and respond consistently, and then mark the N (No), S (Sometimes), or Y (Yes). Your core temperament reflects who you are throughout your life, so think about each question across your lifetime, not just who you are now.

Bulldozer	NO	Sometimes	Yes
1. When presented with a challenge in relationships, do you consider it, accept it, and move on? Do you react without considering your partner's opinion?			
2. Do you feel driven to take the initiative in a relationship?			
3. Do people refer to you as insensitive to their feelings?			
4. Is it easier to control rather than listen, support or converse about the matter?			
5. Are you a visionary, able to see goals clearly?			
6. Are you a workaholic?			
7. Do you like to direct your relationships, both personal and professional?			
8. Does your partner say you are a manipulator?			
9. Do you daydream often about the big game or great activities you love?			
10. Do you work best by yourself?			
11. Do you find it difficult to listen to your partner's feelings or story telling?			
12. If a plan doesn't go your way, is your tendency to get angry?			
13. Do you find it hard to praise others or offer constructive feedback?			
14. Do you like a partner who is a helpful teammate?			
15. Are you a hero who will make it to the top regardless?			
16. Do you feel your partner challenges you in a positive way?			
17. Do people refer to you as emotionally distant?			
18. Is completing or accomplishing your objective important to you?			
19. Do you value highly the rewards of all your efforts?			
20. Do others call you petulant or mean?			
ADD YOUR NUMBERS OF N, S, AND Y AND RECORD HERE IN THE APPROPRIATE COLUMN➜			

Detective	**No**	**Sometimes**	**Yes**
1. Are you quick to criticize others in hopes of helping them improve?			
2. Do others describe you as offering too much feedback?			
3. Do others describe you as being impersonal?			
4. Before making decisions, do you delay so you can research and find more information?			
5. Do you like to be right, or often think you are right, when dealing with people?			
6. Are you a people-watcher, content to sit and observe those around you?			
7. Are you intolerant of others who don't follow instructions or rules?			
8. Do others refer to you as inflexible?			
9. Do you feel over-burdened?			
10. Is it difficult to ask for help from others?			
11. Are you comfortable working with team members when there is order?			
12. Do you prefer to stay out of the spotlight of leadership, and guide and support from behind the scenes?			
13. Do you have difficulty when people reject your ideas?			
14. Do you prefer intimacy with one person rather than being in a group activity?			
15. Do people suggest you could more aware of your feelings or emotions?			
16. Do you have difficulty handling negative emotions, either your own or others?			
17. Do people refer to you as "too sensitive" or "overly sensitive"?			
18. Are you empathic, that is, able to sense or feel other's emotions, ideas or intentions?			
19. Are you respected for your expertise and knowledge?			
20. Is it important for others to acknowledge you for your what you know and do?			
ADD YOUR NUMBERS OF N, S, AND Y AND RECORD HERE IN THE APPROPRIATE COLUMN➔			
Border Collie	**No**	**Sometimes**	**Yes**
1. Do others refer to you as dependable and helpful?			
2. Do you prefer long-term dependable relationships rather than meeting new people or dating around?			
3. Are you sensitive to your environment?			
4. Do you move away from relationships with people who are unkind or negative?			

	No	Sometimes	Yes
5. Are you empathic, actually aware of or feel other's pain or predicaments?			
6. Do others refer to you as tolerant or patient?			
7. Do you feel a powerful need to be accepted by others?			
8. Do others tend to take advantage of you?			
9. Are you gullible or too trusting of other people?			
10. Do you get depressed easily?			
11. Do you pull away from people who offer you help when you get depressed or feel unworthy?			
12. Are you prone to headaches, stomach problems or recurrent issues like colds or allergies?			
13. Are you able to retreat from busyness now and then to renew your energy and focus?			
14. Do your strengths include peacemaking and the ability to negotiate?			
15. Do you feel others take you for granted sometimes?			
16. Do you feel burdened by expectations?			
17. Do you prefer to be comfortable and secure rather than famous?			
18. Do you need to be more assertive or to stand up for yourself?			
19. Do you enjoy creative activities as in cooking, scrapbooking, or another endeavor?			
20. Do others refer to you as accommodating and helpful?			
ADD YOUR NUMBERS OF N, S, AND Y AND RECORD HERE IN THE APPROPRIATE COLUMN➔			

Ringmaster	**No**	**Sometimes**	**Yes**
1. Do others refer to you as enthusiastic and cheerful?			
2. Do you like to express your verbal or artistic abilities?			
3. Do other people refer to you as inspiring to them?			
4. Do you dream of being an actor, dancer, famous author, musician, artist, or public speaker?			
5. Do people say that you are different and march to a different rhythm?			
6. Are you highly intuitive?			
7. Do you get lost in time or lose track of time in your creative projects?			
8. Do you seek stimulation and pleasure?			
9. Do you overindulge in fads, foods, adventure and other such things?			
10. Are you the person who knows rules were made to be broken?			
11. Do you worry much about what other people think?			
12. Have other people called you selfish or insensitive to their needs?			

13. Is your freedom to think and act differently important to you?			
14. Are you focused on the process of living but not always concerned about the end result?			
15. Do you like to move and exercise, finding it difficult to sit still?			
16. Do you deny health issues and don't like doctors?			
17. Are you an entrepreneurial spirit, finding it difficult to fit into the "institutional" or "corporate" structures?			
18. Do you prefer relationships with people who are more like you than different?			
19. Are you distracted and find it hard to establish goals or follow through on promises?			
20. In general, do you feel a deeper sense of isolation from others?			
ADD YOUR NUMBERS OF N, S, AND Y AND RECORD HERE IN THE APPROPRIATE COLUMN➔			

How to Interpret Your Scores

Once you've finished the assessments for each of the core temperaments, transfer your totals to the table below. Then highlight the column that received the highest number of "Yes" answers. This will be your primary core temperament. Remember that each of us has some blend of each of the four core temperaments in our personality. The "Sometimes" column will refer to your secondary temperament. The "No" column shows which temperament has the least influence in your life.

Core Temperaments	No	Sometimes	Yes
Bulldozer			
Detective			
Border Collie			
Ringmaster			

Primary Tendency (Score 16-20) – If your score for a core temperament is in this range, then that core temperament is your dominant or primary tendency or predisposition. The score implies that you are less flexible and more fixed in your temperament. As you repair relationships, you may need to learn to defend less and be more open to feedback and ideas for change. This role is the comfortable pair of slippers that fits you best, and it is the fundamental point of view from which you'll review your preferences for learning, time, people, and information.

Secondary Tendency (Score 10-15) – If your score a core temperament is in this range, consider yourself well-versed in this predisposed temperament. Your secondary core temperament can be supportive of and adaptable to the primary role. This secondary role is like a pair of new shoes that you wear out into the world, where you wouldn't wear your slippers: like a persona that you created as you grew up and adapted to situations, learning how to respond and behave appropriately.

Three or four Close Scores – The more similar scores you have, the more adaptable you have learned to be in all the variety of your environments. This can serve or not serve you depending upon your core strength. Do you blow around like the wind, wondering who you are, and following others - or do you know who you are in the world, have solid boundaries, and tend to lead rather than follow?

Remember: the more equal the scores, the more open and flexible you are; you need to determine whether this will help you or hinder you.

An investment banker had four fairly equal scores, and indeed, he was one of the most adaptable people you could know: friends to everyone, shared knowledge freely, and paid it forward. He had many friends - and yet when he came home at the end of the day, he was a lonely person and felt misunderstood. Rightly so—he blended in so well that he didn't understand himself.

On the other hand, Theo was an only child who was given every opportunity. But his parents were mystified by Theo's ability to dive into playing the piano, seem obsessed by it for a year or two, and then abruptly switch to another instrument until he tired of playing with it. The creative side of Theo yearned to learn an instrument - and then grew bored with it, much like a child who tires of eating macaroni and cheese every day for lunch wants a peanut butter sandwich. Theo seemed to live through his Ringmaster years, and then when he attended the State University, his Detective was activated. He loved science and became a professor at a university. The thrills of discovery of science captivated him for years. In his forties, Theo felt he had missed out on being of service to others. He entered a theological seminary and attended to others' needs as a pastor for the next 15 years, during which time we met and interviewed Theo to hear the remarkable story of how he had lived through three of his four core temperaments - like experiencing three lifetimes in one.

Other Core Predispositions Related to Temperament: Your Learning Preferences

Your learning preference tells you how best to receive and process incoming information from your particular environment. Some people have one strong sense that defines how they experience the world. Others have mixed preferences.

Temperaments	Prefers Direct Experience	Prefers Visual Approaches	Prefers Auditory	Prefers Feeling
Bulldozer	Hands-on, can do it, trial & error approach, achieves and competes			
Detective		Observes, notices, watches, looks, envisions imagery, makes mental lists, processes visual detail.		
Border Collie			Listens, hears, attends to, aware of auditory stimuli, turns attention to	
Ringmaster				Feels, senses, touches, affected by other's feelings, sensation, intuits, aware of energy
The Composite You: Write in your learning preferences and add this to your profile notes				

Knowing this information can help you repair relationships.

You will discover how the person you're observing talks – does he or she use words like think, see, hear, imagine, feel, do, achieve, visualize, create, sense, or know? Each word portrays how someone processes the information that comes to him or her. If you want to reach them, you need to use their language. Likewise, you need to observe your own language and activities to see if you say: I see, I think, I hear, I feel, or I am going to do... In this way you develop the self-awareness you will need to discover if you communicate clearly or if your words miss the mark. You will know if your language is confusing for others if you don't feel heard or find that others don't get what you say.

Knowing your learning preferences allows you to understand and learn to address others in ways that ensure they "get" it. Read the chart on page 33 and take note of which learning preference fits your pattern of response. Note which temperament you identify with in the space provided at the bottom of the chart. This will help you to complete your personal profile.

Core Stress Responses

Dinner is cooking, and the doorbell rings for your package delivery. Your partner is trying to get the grocery list from you on the telephone, but you cannot hear. The dog continues his furious barking because the doorbell is ringing, and you are supposed to be on your weekly conference call right now.

Stressful scenarios like these happen regularly in families and households. It is important to know how you react to stress so you can stop for a moment, regroup, notice, and breathe instead of screaming at the delivery person or the partner buying groceries. These stressful times are a part of every day, and we need to learn to manage them as best we can.

Very few people understand that stressors stem from the needs of their inner core. Like the acorn that provides the blueprint for the majestic oak tree, your core temperament predisposes you to handle stressors in certain ways, and the environment you live in influences you also. Your blueprint survives harsh weather, daily workloads, family arguments, and broken hearts because everyone in the human community experiences such events. Your core needs, if not acknowledged and nourished consistently, influence your behavior dramatically. Your response to stress can be

- Overly defensive.

- Always looking over your shoulder.

- Never feeling safe.

- Repeatedly explaining yourself.

- Always wishing you were somewhere else.

- Routinely apologizing.

- Brushing emotional people off.

- Overly sensitive to criticism or constructive feedback.

Core stress responses formed when your physical or emotional needs were not met in the early years and more importantly, in times of stress, transition, trauma, or terror. YOU are absolutely the only one who can recognize your core needs and meet those needs. In relationships, this is a natural conversation to have between partners, or parents and children; it is this conversation that frees you to support each other in managing stress in a healthy way.

Core stress responses can certainly empower you to plan for easier transitions when, for example, you change schools, relocate, break up, or are promoted. Knowledge of your own temperament patterns helps you manage and even prevent your stressful responses from interfering with your relationships.

Each of the four core temperaments has basic emotional needs that must be met. Not meeting your basic needs is akin to

- Emotionally starving to death.

- Riding the stress roller coaster and feeling like you can never get off.

- Unconsciously doing the same thing over and over and beating yourself up about it.

- Feeling helpless and overwhelmed by life.

Not having your basic needs met can be terrifying at any age, because the everyday events of life can crush you to dust. On the other hand, you can modify your stress response for your health by adapting your core temperaments to be more closely in tune with your environment. When this happens in a relationship, we've seen magic happen! Suddenly you feel so much better, and those in relationship with you notice and respond very differently than before.

In what part of your life are you most likely to find it necessary to deal with meeting needs? Our core feelings: vulnerable or protected, needy or fulfilled, are definitively revealed in relationships. You know which combination of the core temperaments is your nature. In the chart on page 35 you will find a listing of

1. The truth about your inner needs.
2. What causes your stress.
3. How you might react.
4. What you can do to care for yourself.

In the far right column, personalize your profile even further: write down your true inner core needs and how you react to stress, act out your reactions, and repair your own patterns.

In the last row, write down your ideas for how to take care of your own needs. This is an important requirement before you move into relationship repair by asking a partner or friend to assist and serve in the capacity of that one trustworthy person you can count on to help you by listening, escaping to a quiet spa or hockey game, keeping you grounded so you don't worry, or going to the gym with you to work off excess energy.

Defining Your Core Temperament's Needs, Stressors and Reactions

	Bulldozer	**Border Collie**	**Detective**	**Ringmaster**	**Composite You**
Core Needs	Achievement Challenge Mastery Control Support	Appreciation Agreement Caring Belonging Connection	Structure Detail Respect Quality Safety	Admiration Influence Freedom Expression of ideas Value	
Stressors	• When others are too slow or can't keep up • When efforts are blocked • When challenged for control • When others are overly talkative or emotional	• When others are angered or mean • When taken advantage of • When judged • When others are unjust	When others… • Rush them • Show disrespect • Show emotionality • Have unclear communication	When others… • Are focused on things and tasks, not people • Limit freedom • Ignore them • Compete for attention • Are critical	
Reaction	Becomes moody Sulks Acts out Withdraws in anger Becomes persistent	Gets depressed Withdraws Suffers silently Holds it in Feels uncared for	Worries, goes to head to think about options, feels unsafe, withdraws, maybe hides as thoughts of future seem dim	Wants to escape Seeks attention elsewhere Pretends not to care Laughs it off Moves on	
Self Care					

We have given you a revealing look at your core self, how you typically handle stress, and how to define your learning preferences. There are two more spicy ingredients that we'd like you to add to your self-awareness. The first ingredient is values. We think of values as similar to those Champion Jordan Air Nike shoes that provide strong foundations, a superb cushion, and the power to move and win. Values are the foundation of your goals, achievements, and desires. Your core temperament comes with a built-in set of values that guide you to the winning dunk in the basket or keep your feet firmly on your path. Here's the kicker: if you don't know what your values are, then you plow ahead in life, tripping over rocks you can't see, being taken advantage of, and feeling your gut twist and turn in warning.

Knowing your values can save you anguish: they can head off poor decisions and impulsive behavior. How? You determine what your values are and then you check in with your three voices of HUG to make sure you are aligned with *your* truth, no one else's. In this book, you start with being true to yourself!

Your values = your choices = your destiny = your responsibility.

A brief review of what you've learned about yourself so far.

Take the time now to go back over what you've discovered about yourself. Write it here.

My primary core temperament is:	
My secondary core temperament is:	
What I have learned about how I react and interact with people is:	
My learning preference is:	
What I would like to improve in my relationships is:	

Chapter Three

Values: The Second Tool in the Relationship Repair System

Embrace and incorporate these powerful values, and you will start living with more integrity, honesty, compassion and enthusiasm. This, in turn, will breathe new life into your relationship.

~Dr. Phil

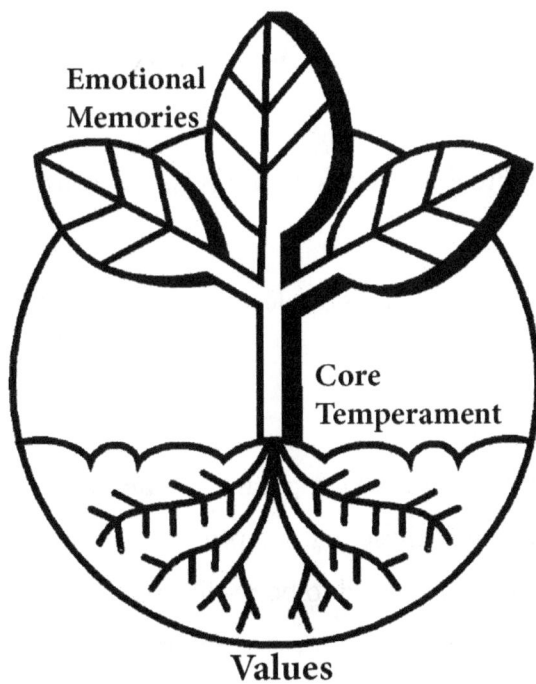

Emotional Memories

Core Temperament

Values

Values are the cornerstone of your relationships and determine what you believe about money, free time, work, friends, intimacy, clothes, politics, family, and spirituality. Values drive your actions and add meaning to your life. One of your essential roles in relationships is to identify your values: first as an individual and then together if in an intimate relationship. Values are the first thread you will use to determine what you have in common or where you clash in your relationships - whether in the kitchen, with your children, or at work.

Jennifer, a single mom, values time and efficiency; she works hard for her paycheck. Her sixteen-year-old son values his freedom and time on weekends with his music. They clash when it comes to getting chores done on time. Jennifer does not argue with her son about chores: she has worked out a contract with her him for three hours of time, Friday through Sunday, when he contributes to cooking, cleaning, and laundry.

When you understand how your values influence your choices, you'll want to take a heart-centered approach to relationships and communication because you'll learn how to make better choices.

Luke is fifty-two years old and wants to marry a bright light, Ingrid, who he has been dating for eight months. His wife passed away two years ago. Two of his adult children are married and a third is in school. Ingrid makes him feel so alive again that he would like to start a second family with her.

Ingrid, a professional trainer, travels for her work two weeks out of every month. At the age of 39, she has already determined she does not want children and feels Luke is the perfect spouse.

He values intimacy and the security of close family ties. She values her independence and freedom. Their values clash but they are both emotionally stable adults who need to do more than just talk about their situation. They need to use the HUG alignment process to identify their mutual concerns and show them the path to a happy marriage that includes and satisfies the values of both.

Examples of values can include honesty, security, abundance, gratitude, respect, communication, knowledge, love, happiness, harmony, trust, reliability, responsibility, spirituality, faith, loyalty, or truthfulness. We are focusing on the values that are truly important to us in our relationships.

- The **Bulldozer** would like to be supported in her challenge so her partner runs alongside her for the first leg of a marathon run.

- A **Detective** feels safe in an intimate relationship: one that has grown over time. He values friendship and loyalty.

- The **Border Collie** enjoys it when people notice and appreciate the small things she does for her family and friends.

- The **Ringmaster** feels passionately alive when sharing with others the sales process, the information he has learned or the training he can deliver.

The chart on page 39 offers the values associated with the four core temperaments and indicates where each value is likely to show up as behavior. Incorporate any of these that are prominent in your life. We would like you to know which values are part of your core and need to be re-discovered to help you prioritize your decisions and needs. Then, in the next section, take the values inventory, compare this with the core temperament list and choose those values that are relevant to your relationships right now.

Just as you have a core temperament, you also have a set of values which are easily identified and prioritized for you to make the best decisions; these values feel right to your gut, your heart, and your head. Imagine the freedom of knowing that you are making accurate decisions and never have to look back or think twice!

Do you remember a time when you made a wrong decision to lie - to skip a day from work and call in sick? When you examine that decision you'll see that you knew what you were doing was wrong - like buying alcohol in high school - but you did it anyway. The voice inside that made you feel guilty or reminded you the action was wrong was your core value voice speaking.

The Values Associated with Your Core Temperament

Core temperaments	Values	Shows Up In
Bulldozer	Stimulation	Need to achieve
	Challenge	Likes the reward
	Responsibility	Likes to be in charge
	Accomplishment	Likes self-sufficiency
	Power	Authority to act
Detective	Intimacy	Need for structure
	Instruction	Need for respect
	Order	Need for understanding
	Expertise	Need for completeness
	Perfection	Need for recognition
Border Collie	Being acknowledged	Need for appreciation
	Peace	Need for agreement
	Teamwork	Need for caring
	Safety	Need for steadfastness
	Common Sense	Need for inner atisfaction
Ringmaster	Friendship	Likes influencing others
	Being admired	Wants to be center of attention
	Ingenuity	Expression of ideas
	Pleasure	Recreation
	Freedom	Travel/change

Which Ones Ring True?

Take a minute to write down your primary and secondary core temperaments. Note which of the associated values feels important to you. It's okay if not all of them resonate with you, just write down the ones that you feel the strongest pull towards.

Primary Core Temperament:

Values:

Secondary Core Temperament:

Values:

You can of course ignore the truth about what you value but the voice never really goes away. To help you to strengthen your values, you'll next determine what you value or feel strongly about.

Know what you value as an individual.

Living a values-based life is equivalent to living a heart-centered life.

Your values hover in the background of your thoughts and emotions as ghostly reminders of what you believe is important: you'll recognize them as strong desires that motivate you and lead you to action. We have found that you can identify your true-to-you core values by asking yourself the following questions. Record your responses in a journal.

What are the priorities in your intimate relationships?

Examples include education, fitness, health, love, happiness, and adventure.

In Brad's family, music education is important: how does that play out in practice? His 12-year-old son is learning to play the upright bass with a passion. His 10-year-old daughter takes piano lessons and joined the drum club at her elementary school. Brad encourages the kids to play for fun, but also wants them to practice daily to develop consistent habits that will build their playing skills.

If fitness is something you value highly, you will encourage long walks or shared exercise sessions with your partner or even a coworker.

Minette's family loves long walks at a local nature preserve on Sunday mornings.

Summary: The first way to recognize what you value is that you enjoy it, feel passionate about it, and enjoy sharing it with those in your relational sphere. Your values are the grease on the grill that makes your life sizzle: the buzz starts inside when you are on the path to something right on and right up your alley. This is proactive living.

- If you never experience the sizzle, then you are not feeling the fire of your values.

- If you are not feeling the fire, the reason could be that you are busy being angry, upset, or defensive about what you do value, as though no one gets it like you do, can do it as well as you do, or just doesn't appreciate your talent and empathy. Answer the next question in depth to find and define your values.

Identify the behaviors that bug you.

Other people's actions or choices that bug you provide clues to your values. For example, your own value system includes strong feelings about the behavior of those around you. If integrity is number one on the list of your core values, then people who lie disturb you deeply. If you value results, you find it stressful to deal with people who don't follow through. If you respect people's time and keep appointments on the hour, you might consider someone who is always late as disrespectful to you personally, as opposed to understanding it could be a part of their core temperament. Sometimes actions that bug you the most can cause you to work hard for a good cause because your emotional memories have triggered your sense of injustice.

Caron's mom could never hit her children unless truly angered, and that only happened once. If one of her six children misbehaved or lied outright, mom made all six kids sit in the bathroom, waiting for their dad to come home and use the belt. All the kids knew which one was the guilty party, but no one would tattle, so everyone was spanked with the belt over dad's knee. This sense of injustice, learned as a child being spanked when her twin brothers were usually the instigators became a crusade when Caron heard a parent threaten a child in public or watched a parent beat a child for having tantrums in the grocery store. Caron values nurturing children and seeking out the cause behind the child's behavior to alleviate symptoms rather than using physical violence to discipline them, thus showing them disrespect rather than helping them to overcome their problems.

Summary: When someone's speech or actions annoy you, list "this bugs me because I disagree with _____ and value _____." Another way to say it is "this person (or this action) bothers me because in the past I remember_____. Remembering now helps me transform my irritable or angry feelings into action like _____."

How do you choose to spend your time?

Do you spend time working, cleaning house, having fun, seeking adventure, being creative, cultivating laughter, reading, or praying? We recently participated in a business mastermind session in which we discussed what we value and how we spend our time. The leader of the group said, "Show me your check book and I will show you where you spend your time." Think about it. If you say you value saving money or eating healthy food or exercising, but really you are antique shopping, eating out, and running up credit card debt, you are internally at odds with your core values.

Where in your life are you not being true to yourself? Where does this show up in your relationships?

Identifying & Prioritizing Your Values in Relationships

On page 44 you will find a list of possible values. To assess what your values are, follow the steps listed. Think about each word in the context of the answers you gave to the questions in the last section: what bugs you; what are your priorities; how do you choose to spend your time. Also take into consideration the values affiliated with your core temperament as outlined in the chart on page 39. You should do this on your own first and then with your partner, kids, or coworkers. You'll compare and contrast your values and prioritize two lists. The first is your personal list of values that guide your choices and the second might be a list of family values or professional values. Your list can include two options:

> a. Non-negotiable Values are values you will not compromise or be willing to change because they are important to you.

> b. Negotiable Values are values that you are willing to modify and prioritize together with the set of values held by your partner, kids or coworkers.

Your Core Values Assessment

Instructions

1. Using the list on page 44 put a circle around all of the words that you feel are important, right, or necessary. Circle up to 30 words on the list that are meaningful to you. Don't think about it. Just start circling! Give yourself several minutes to do this.

2. Next, go back and put a star next to half of the listed words that are the most meaningful to you. These words are the core of what is important and what defines right or wrong for you.

3. Finally, narrow down that list by underlining, highlighting or marking ten of the words. These words drive you, internally motivate your decision-making process, and define you as a person.

The key here is to drill down to the critical core of who you are from a values-based perspective. Note that on your original lists from steps two and three, you probably found words that were important to your family, your community, or your church that feel like "shoulds."

Your goal is to create a very clear mental image of what matters to you in your relationships, both personal and professional. If you have a solid list for each type of relationship, then even better! Our values can shift between work and home. Trust your heart and trust your gut because values elicit strong feelings.

If you are in a marriage or committed relationship, your partner needs to define his/her core values, independent of yours. You would do the same when creating values around how you want to parent your children.

Understanding what is important to you will help you see where you are similar and where you differ from your partner in everything from intimacy and parenting to bigger themes like money, time, stress, security, spirituality, and work ethic. When you have this information, you'll work together to choose a list of values that reflects the best of both of you and mirrors the vision of the relationship that you want to create.

If you are single, you might talk to other single friends or your parents about your list and why it's important to you. It's great to have a sounding board in a good friend who will listen to your aspirations and ask you thoughtful questions about why these values matter in your relationships.

Together, you and your spouse/partner will now compare your lists and agree on 10 values that are central to what you want to create as a family.

Your Core Values Combined

Minette and Brad said that creating and having this final thought-provoking list to discuss as a couple and as a family strengthened their relationship. They worked with a life coach, who walked them through their process and moderated the heated discussion over what was most important, but you can easily do it on your own. You have to be open and honest with each other. While their discussion was at times energetic, it was also collaborative and never angry. They both had the same goal: "A list of ten values that forms the core of our parenting and our life together."

Instructions

Step One. Get a giant piece of paper and markers (we used large art paper, but you could use anything you have at hand. A white board would work well, also.) Assign one person to do the writing. Write a list of the words and concepts that you feel

- Define you as individuals or

- Are important to you in raising your children and growing as a family or

- Define your business.

Use the list of ten values you chose from the exercise in the last section as a starting point. Have the entire list available as new values may arise when you consider your family or relationship.

Partial Core Values List

For a printable version of this list go to: http://www.heartwiserelationships.com

Accomplishment	Diversity	Ingenuity	Rule of Law
Accountability	Ease of Use	Justice	Safety
Accuracy	Efficiency	Knowledge	Satisfying others
Acknowledgement	Equality	Leadership	Security
Adventure	Excellence	Love, Romance	Self-giving
All for one & one for all	Expertise	Loyalty	Self-reliance
Authenticity	Fairness	Mastery	Self-thinking
Beauty	Faith	Meaning	Service to others
Calm, quietude, peace	Faithfulness	Merit	Seeing clearly
Challenge	Family	Methodical	Simplicity
Change	Family feeling	Money	Skill
Cleanliness, orderliness	Flair	Openness	Solving Problems
Collaboration	Freedom	Order	Speed
Commitment	Friendship	Originality	Spirit in life (using)
Common Sense	Fun	Patriotism	Spirituality
Communication	Genius	Peace, Non-violence	Stability
Community	Global view	Perfection	Standardization
Competence	Good will	Personal Growth	Status
Competition	Goodness	Pleasure	Stimulation
Concern for others	Gratitude	Power	Strength
Connection	Hard work	Practicality	Succeed; a will to-
Content over form	Harmony	Preservation	Success
Continuous improvement	Health	Privacy	Systemization
Cooperation	Honesty	Progress	Teamwork
Coordination	Honor	Prosperity, Wealth	Timeliness
Courage	Improvement	Punctuality	Tolerance
Creativity	Independence	Quality of work	Tradition
Customer satisfaction	Individuality	Regularity	Tranquility
Decisiveness	Inner peace, calm, quietude	Reliability	Trust
Delight of being, joy	Innovation	Resourcefulness	Truth
Democracy	Integrity	Respect for others	Unity
Discipline	Intensity	Responsiveness	Variety
Discovery	Intimacy	Results-oriented	Wisdom

Minette and her husband Brad made some interesting discoveries. For example, Brad put <u>fun</u> on his list. Being the more serious of the two, it had not occurred to Minette to even declare fun as a value. After listening to Brad's explanation of why he valued fun, she realized that he was right. Now that they have defined, explored and embraced it, fun has become an important part of their family life.

Step Two. Once you have at least 20 words on the page(s), use your marker to circle or star the most important values. Whittle your list down to ten key values that define your core as a couple or a family. Be prepared to explain to your partner why each value matters to you. These core values can serve as your moral compass in a romantic, loving relationship. You can imagine how Minette's understanding that her husband needed more fun in their relationship changed her perspective of him and allowed them to interact in new ways. They now enjoy finding ways to have more fun together and explore how they experience fun differently.

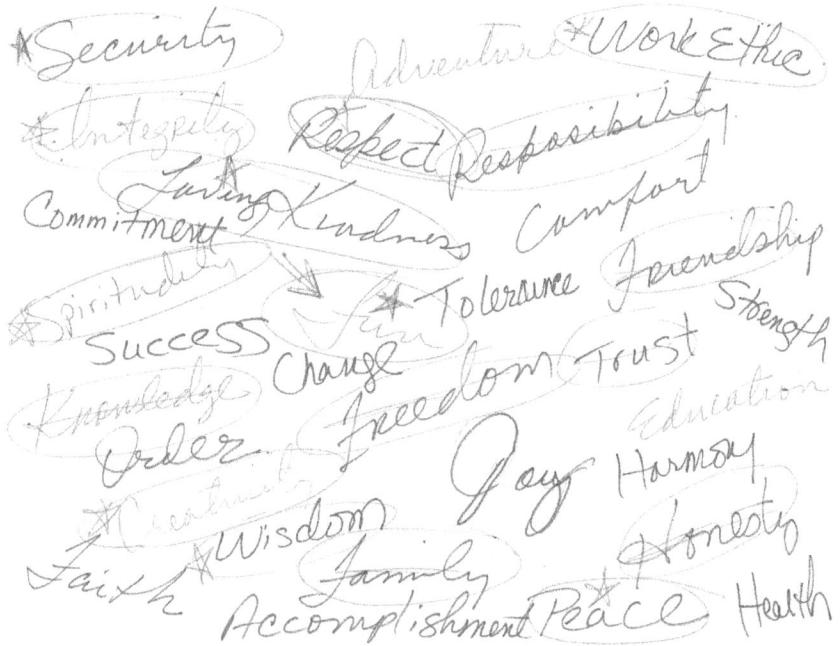

Step Three. Transfer your values in order of importance to a clean sheet of paper. Brad and Minette typed their list on card stock and posted it near the kitchen table where they eat, so that the kids also see the values daily. Here is their list in order of importance to them: integrity, respect, loving kindness, wisdom, peace, creativity, spirituality, security, work ethic, and fun.

Please note that fun ended up being last on the list, but it is there. They worked hard to prioritize the list in a way that was meaningful to their lives and their beliefs.

One of the challenges you face is that if, after you do all this work (coming up with a great list of values and getting excited about how it can help you), you stick it in a drawer and forget about it. Keeping your values visible helps overcome this challenge of obscurity.

One last note: the list of 10 core values you are creating does not infer that other values are not important as well. We all have different ideas, emotions, and feelings attached to a variety of values. Don't feel that you are limited to the top ten: just be clear that values you choose are true to you and your core temperament and not values you feel you "should" adopt because of race, religion, politics, community, or culture.

Write your list of 10 core values here with a few words about why they matter to you:

1. _____

2. _____

3. _____

4. _____

5. _____

6. _____

7. _____

8. _____

9. _____

10. _____

How Values Assist Your Relationship Repair

Now that you know what your values are, this is how they help you in relationship repair. First, your values guide your decisions. You ask yourself questions about the issues you are unsure about in this way:

- Is dating this person in alignment with my value of harmony, or love, or adventure?

- Am I keeping my integrity by going to this party or participating in that action? Can I live with myself in the morning?

- In keeping with my value of independence, is now the best time to have children?

- Does staying in this job support my values or limit my values?

- Does investing this money feel in alignment with my head, heart, and gut?

- Does taking this action compromise my value or cause my gut to twinge or my heart to feel odd or different?

- Is there something I am not seeing? Is there a point I need to be aware of?

Summary: Values are the guardrails on your highway of life, and they keep you from veering too far off the shoulder. They help you focus and define the most empowering choices to enhance your journey, whether your goal is passion, parenting, being a professional, or simply living with a purpose.

Action Values for Relations Repair

A loving relationship is one in which the loved one is free to be himself — to laugh with me, but never at me; to cry with me, but never because of me; to love life, to love himself, to love being loved. Such a relationship is based upon freedom and can never grow in a jealous heart.

-Leo F. Buscaglia

You are hard-wired for relationships, and this book makes clear that you also come hard-wired with predispositions that remain your core throughout life. The image of the tree portrays well the strength of your core and your ability to adapt in varied environments. The roots of the tree provide your anchored foundation, with the flexibility to grow and adapt in a variety of environments. The trunk of the tree also bends, blows or falls according to the emotional weathering of erupting anger, spewing ash, blow-hard arrogance, emotional tremors of tears, or birth quakes of personal realization. Values feed you and keep you steady or on your feet when your world explodes.

There is no doubt that trauma, tension, anxiety and stress can trigger you into old emotions. Since you know that emotional memories are replays of a different age and time, we suggest that you let values be the roots you rest on to regroup.

- When inside you hurt prevails, you can still take control of your outer environment.

- When the outer world is shattered, you can still control your inner emotions and responses.

- In either case, values will be your glue because they are your deep-held beliefs and support your core resilience in tough times. They are your roots!

- If you feel lost or defeated, values help you remember who YOU are.

Kathy was devastated to learn that Rick, her husband of four years, had a brief sexual fling with his work colleague, a woman whom Kathy met once at an office party. He said the fling meant nothing, and Kathy's heart ached because she wanted to believe him, but she couldn't. She knew that Rick saw the woman every day.

Kathy sat down to review the list of values that Rick and she drew up after a HeartWise Values Workshop. Trust was at the top of her list. Trust wasn't on Rick's list because he said that it was a given, a part of him already, and he didn't need to add it to the list they were making together.

She felt an instant disconnect from Rick, as if an icy hand had slapped her face. Kathy realized that with her Border Collie temperament, she was prone to trusting people too much, and she expected the same from others. If she found an untrustworthy person or felt that a friend or colleague in her sphere of friends didn't show her respect, she moved out of that circle. How was she going to handle this now?

Like Kathy, you may face an important choice, and the choice comes down to either feeling in alignment with yourself or staying out of alignment to be with another - doing what they want, not speaking up, and eventually feeling used and pulled in unhappy directions.

You'll feel authentic when you are true to your deepest values, distressed when you're indifferent to them, ashamed when you have disregarded them, and meaningless when you lose touch with them.

Mine? Yours? Or Ours?

When values clash and differences blow up in your face, you are all you have. You can only change yourself and choose the values that keep you whole and your integrity intact. Only then are you ready to bring the values to the table for discussion.

At the same time, you want to insure that your emotions are not hijacking you, and you are clear enough emotionally to review your values for EACH situation.

First, calmness begins in the heart. Placing your right hand on your heart, ask your body if you are calm enough to review each of your values and rate its importance in the situation.

When Kathy was sure that emotional memories weren't clouding her vision, she rated the values that related to Rick's fling on a 5-point scale. 1 was the lowest relevance and 5 was the highest relevance of her values to the event

1. Respect – 5
2. Trust – 5
3. Communication about the event – 4

Rick also compiled his top 3 values to discuss:

1. Truth - 5
2. Respect - 4
3. Freedom - 5

The discussion between Rick and Kathy concluded with Rick valuing his freedom and also feeling guilty enough not to lie to Kathy. He said he respected her, but Kathy called him on his lack of alignment. "You cannot say you respect me, and then feel guilty and dump your fling on me," she cried.

"I do respect you, but the fling was an act of freedom. I fell into it because of pressures at work. It wasn't about you." Rick tried to explain his position, justifying the action through his values.

"Yes, it is about me, and whether you were acting out some suppressed teen crap or you still want to escape under pressure, there are other ways to escape. What you did was selfish and impulsive. You have shown me that I can't trust you to control your impulses."

After a long silence, Rick concluded, *"You're right Kath. My inclination is to be impulsive when pressured. If I don't, I explode. A few drinks at the party and all self-respect was lost."* Rick recognized the truth of his core temperament's response: to escape under stress. He came to see that his drinking hindered his clarity.

At least this couple kept their dialogue open to further defining the values they could share for their actions while continuing to respect each other.

Value As A Verb

Rick was not as in touch as Kathy was to the ways values could be called on to provide guidelines for his behavior. Seeing Kathy stick to her values impressed him: he saw her strength. Her insistence that he was completely out of alignment in his relationship offered him a choice: damaging his marriage or earning once again the trust she placed in him when she said, "I do."

What was the difference between Kathy's and Rick's use of their values? Kathy described it this way:

"When I write respect on my list of values, to me it is not a word that I look at or try to remember. I write down the verb, 'I respect…' and list those people in my life to whom I wish to show respect."

The way you write down your values reflects their usefulness to you. Rick wrote down words to please his partner and put the list in his desk.

Value as noun	Value as verb	How to live it
Love	I love…	I am loving toward
Friendship	I befriend	I am a friendly person
Humor	I'll infuse my blog with humor	I look for humor in others
Spirituality	I meditate and connect to my inner spirit	I wake each morning with a grateful spirit prepared for the coming day.

The significance of any value is in *your* context. If you value someone, you elevate that person in your view. If you value an activity, you do it because it is enjoyable. Values are revealed through your experiences. Because Rick had never respected a woman personally or held a woman in high regard, the value of respect was not strong enough within him to check his impulsivity.

You are a better person when you learn, appreciate, protect, better yourself, connect, bond, share, or make a commitment. You expand into a well-rounded person, become flexible and more open when good relationships support you.

Four Core Values That Foster Good Relationships

In our personal and professional relationships we have identified a set of basic core values that we present as guides for all relationships, whether parenting, partners, or friends. In the world of relationships, these four values are words of action, not just a mental representation of some nice thing. Since values are abstract to many people, here is the way you as adults in relationships can make values work with your friends, children, colleagues or lovers. View these values as sequenced strategies for repairing relationships.

Connection – to be linked or bonded with another person or people. When a child is born, the bonding process involves sight, touch, empathy and positive regard. Empathy is established through eye contact and touch which programs the child's brain to recognize, connect, and feel the parent or caregiver. Empathy and positive regard for the child are also connected through conversation, cuddling, holding, and movement (walking and rocking). When a parent treats and speaks to the babe or toddler with kindness, softness, love, and tenderness, the child feels valued and develops an emotional foundation: it begins to feel safe, cherished, respected, and cared for. Our bodies grow and change, but our human needs for connection to and bonding with a loving person never change.

Think of the most horrible anguish a child can experience: feeling abandoned, feeling tiny and disrespected through being yelled at, treated like an object, dismissed, hit, screamed at, and threatened. These traumatic events are emotional memories in the making, and they will surely hijack this child as an adult.

Do you think adults feel any different? Each core temperament has needs to be met, and when they are not met, the pattern for emotional abandonment is triggered. You are hard-wired for relationships; feeling connected is a priority for communication and commitment.

Review your needs from the core temperament chart on page 35 and write them here.

Primary Core Temperament:

Secondary Core Temperament:

Question for Your Review: In what ways do you feel connected to those closest to you?

Communication - as a value, communication is more than just sending a message or conversing. As a value, it means to be in rapport with someone or in our language aligned in head, heart and gut. Being aligned with each other in the gut helps you feel safe. Being aligned in the heart helps you feel loved or valued. Being aligned in the head implies no judgment, acceptance and the ability to share, argue, debate, and plan without taking it personally. To be in rapport means you can:

- disagree without being disagreeable,
- make an effort to control your emotional hijacking and not dump on another,
- move away from the need to be right and shift to listening, being open or reflective,
- be objective, even while being emotional.

Question for Your Review: How high do you rank communication as a core value in your relationships? We suggest you make it number 1 on your values list for one month and cultivate this quality within yourself: notice how your relationships improve.

Courage - to be brave – to have guts, audacity, valor, going forth or moving ahead despite fear. We believe that relationships absolutely require guts, especially for you Border Collie types that love harmony and peace, or you Ringmasters who love to escape the pressures of modern relationships. Detectives need courage to face the world: to step into and participate actively in their relationships. Bulldozers: you can be fearless, so you might not believe that you need courage. You might be right in pointing out that your achievements speak to bravery. We feel you might need more courage to be sensitive in your relationships, where you tend to dismiss sensitivity and feelings.

Even if you feel like a total wimp, or like a frightened doormat, list courage as a value. Each morning, repeat your mantra of courage in action.

- I am courage in action.
- I have courage to face…
- I see courage in my eyes.
- My act of courage today will be…

Question for your review – In what ways are you courageous in facing your fears and moving through emotional hijacking situations?

Commitment – to pledge or promise to follow through, accepting a responsibility.

Some core temperament types such as the Bulldozer, Border Collie, or Ringmaster might take commitment more lightly than their partner or child would like. That is because these types might make promises that they can't keep in a reasonable length of time. Bulldozers get caught up in their actions, visions and planning. Border Collies get overwhelmed and tend to put promises on the back burner. Ringmasters shift priorities like the wind and may even forget their commitments if you are out of sight and out of mind.

This happens because all of us have good intentions. You make commitments fully intending to keep them, but…life happens. Those to whom we commit can only assume we have forgotten unless we take some sort of action like communicating, making an action plan or settling on a date for delivery.

When you forget the promise, the person in relation to you can feel belittled by your lack of respect for them. If that is not the outcome that you desire from your relationships, then add a time line to your commitment in order to be more accountable: see our Action Chart on page 106 for guidance.

Responsibility is the twin to Commitment and means that you can be depended upon to follow through and complete tasks or commitments, and to be accountable for doing so.

As a parent or in relationship with a life partner, commitment and responsibility are paramount.

Question for Review: In what ways are you currently demonstrating your commitment to your partner, family or job? Where are you failing to follow through?

Using Values To Prioritize What's Important In Any Relationship

A set of carefully chosen values serves as a personal compass in showing you the right, appropriate, or socially acceptable way to achieve your goals in relationships. Whether you feel like the leader, the follower, or as an equal partner or team player, values are still very personal and do not come with rights and wrongs. When comparing or discussing values with others, all you can do is abide by your values and be aware of what is best for you in this relationship.

We are discussing your personal values in this context, not the moral or cultural values that have been established in society, religions, and institutions where we work and receive education. All of us agree that these social rules are present and serve as a behavioral guideline for all human behavior. You may or may not consider them significant in living with an intimate partner or rearing children. As we've shown you previously, the determining of personal values for families and businesses are group discussions that require compromise and collaboration.

Defining values is not an easy task: we learn about our values when a person or a situation leaves us feeling uncomfortable, hurt, abandoned, and not respected. This is precisely the time to go to the HUG technique taught in Section IV: it gives you time to feel aligned and discover where the relevant emotional memory can be discovered and worked with. This is an opportunity to define our values so we can use them in a proactive manner in each of our relationships.

We suggest you have one worksheet for each relationship: Intimate Partner, Child(ren), Relative or family member, Friend, Professional Colleague.

The chart below asks you to evaluate each relationship in four steps:

1. Review the relationship with the person in your mind, and let the general flavor and feeling of the relationship come through.

2. Review the feelings and images related to the relationship and write down the ones you like.

3. Write down the qualities you do like about the individual.

4. Draw a conclusion based on your observations – is the relationship supportive, connected, based on friendship and respect, mutually happy, mutually satisfying? Does it fulfill you or drain you? Does it occupy your time and thoughts? Can you be yourself in this relationship? Does it help you grow and stretch? Does it stifle you or hurt you?

After completing these exercises, if one of them leaves you with more questions and doubts than answers, write out your concerns and use the HUG guide in Section IV to make decisions about how to be more authentic in the relationship and how to ensure the relationship supports you.

The person in relationship to you	The qualities you like about the relationship	The qualities you don't like about the relationship	I conclude that this relationship is…
Parenting Partner			
Friend			
Intimate			
Colleague			

In Summary

*   Values are only as real and relevant as you make them. They are the words which remind you that there are supportive and respectful standards that you would like to have in your relationships, especially with your intimate partner and your parenting partner.

- The purpose of values is to help you be clear within yourself; they give you the strength and the courage to mean what you say and stand for what you mean.

- When you are not aligned with your values your heart hurts, your gut acts up, and your mind nags at you – all clear communications from your self to you. Please listen carefully.

- Values are empty words unless you make them action words: I love, I am loving, and I love my child in this way…

- Periodically review the values for each relationship in your circle of influence. Have the courage and commitment to make the changes necessary to stay aligned in your head, heart and gut.

People are lonely because they build walls instead of bridges.
- Joseph F. Newton

Chapter Four

Tool Three Is HUG™

"Consciousness happens when our inner trio plays its tune: our head knows,
our heart feels, our gut agrees." – David Richo.

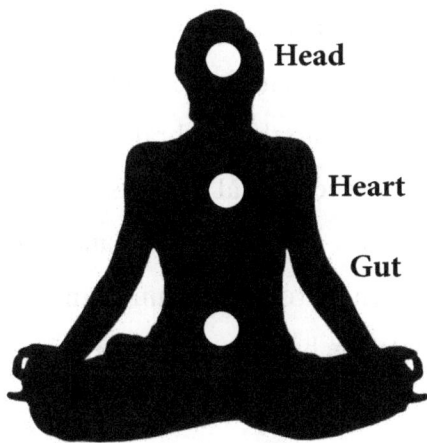

Head

Heart

Gut

Image I

Persons who value rational thinking or those who see through the scientific lens might ignore and even deride the heart's longing for love and the instinctual gut twinge. However, recent research suggests that your heart and your gut are brains in and of themselves. A brain is an organ of thought and feeling, and we'll explain why the heart and the gut are brains or minds, another term used by scientist and author Dr. Candace Pert.

Candace Pert, author of *Molecules of Emotions* learned from her research that the neuropeptides of any emotional feeling travel throughout the body. She uses the term "mind" to indicate that consciousness is not local or specific to the brain in our head, or even our gut. Rather…

Dr. Pert's research provides scientific evidence that a biochemical basis for awareness and consciousness exists, that the mind and body are indeed one, and that our emotions and feelings are the bridge that link the two. She explains, "The chemicals that are running our body and our brain are the same chemicals that are involved in emotion."[1]

Gone are the days of thinking that the head brain is the end-all and be-all of human thinking, feeling, and creativity. You will see that in addition to the organ in our cranium, the heart as well as the gut are organs of thought and feeling, connected to the head brain. The organs and their corresponding nerve ganglia and neuropeptide communication network make them "minds," implying a connected,

[1] http://www.healingcancer.info/ebook/candace-pert

integrated system for attention, awareness, and memory. So if a brain (whether in head, heart or gut) is an organ for thought and feeling, then let us remember that each organ is a complete network of communication connected to all other organs. No "brain" or "mind" stands as separate from another in your body, but the brains in the head, heart, and gut, offer you a unique viewpoint, as well as a voice, to help you solve problems, make key decisions, and repair relationships.

For the purposes of this book, we will use the metaphoric term "brains" to refer to the body area for the head (forehead, crown), heart, (as in chest area) and gut (as in abdomen or navel area). When we suggest you place your hand on that body area or move your awareness to your head, heart or gut we are speaking specifically forehead, chest, and navel centers. Here's how the HHG system works.

Three Brains

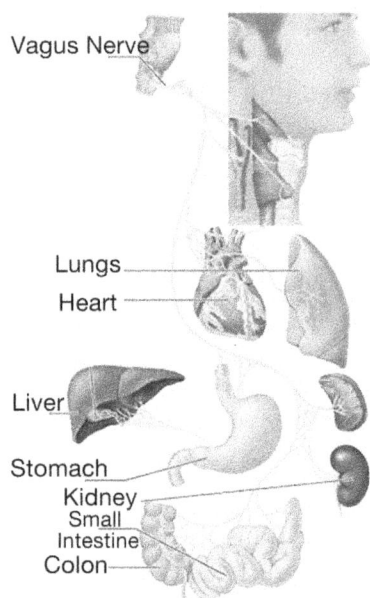

Image II

Your body has 3 brains…in your gut, your heart, and your head. In the fetus, the heart develops first and extends neural tubes forming a primitive intestine and then the brain tissue. During fetal growth, the same layer of tissue extends into the gut brain, enteric nervous system, and also develops into the central nervous system and brain. These brains in the head, heart and gut connect and communicate via the vagus nerve that extends from the brain stem into the abdomen and has extensive reach into the heart and other organs. (See Image II.)

The body is in the mind and the mind is in the body. Dr. Candace Pert stated, "our body is our subconscious mind." To know our deeper thoughts and feelings about relationships, we have to talk to the subconscious part of ourselves within the heart and gut. Often the body "knows" before the head brain even receives a signal. The body can store memories that our mind doesn't remember.

All three brains can influence your behavior, moods, and even thoughts. Over the past two decades research into the human body's three brains is fascinating and reminds us that we are still in the dark ages about how they function but we are learning fast. We know the pulse of the human heart extends to other cells in the body and can have a calming or agitating effect.

Another example is that psychiatrists still treat depression and other mood disorders as chemical imbalances in the brain. Yet researchers find that depression and other behavioral issues appear to be linked to an imbalance of bacteria in the gut. This makes perfect sense if you examine our physiology. Each brain of the trio has a specific function, which dictates the voice or viewpoint you will address in the HUG procedure so can begin to understand your deeper feelings, inspirations, fears, and beliefs.

- The **head brain** observes, reasons, and rationalizes.
- The **heart brain** is the emotional center and stores memories of emotional events: it can be reflective.
- The **gut brain**, an older, more primitive aspect of physiology, serves as the instinctive, intuitive part.

The three brains represent your inner voices of logic, emotion and practical intuition.

- **The head brain, the voice of logic**, is colored by common sense and plans for the future as it looks forward. Reason speaks from the bias of its education, training, culture, religion and parenting. Remember the head brain's knowledge is derived from an accumulation of life experiences, and it will try to protect you from repeating mistakes.
- **The heart brains feels and remembers the emotions**, both pleasant and painful. The heart longs to engage, connect, dream, and perceives that all others can connect at this feeling level. That is the heart's bias. The heart does remember emotional feelings.
- **The gut voice tends to be hands-on practical.** The instinctive gut brain reacts in the moment, present time. The gut has the advantage of evolution that it intuits without bias.

The purpose of the HeartWise HUG™ approach is for you to:

- check in with yourself and find your own answers.
- insure your values and decisions are aligned.
- ask questions when fearful or hesitant.
- tune in and listen to yourself – your thoughts, emotions, feelings.

How to Tune In & Listen

Listening to your three voices takes place this way:

1. Before you ask a question, place your <u>right</u> hand briefly on your forehead, then on your heart, and then on your gut or abdomen. Your hand is feeling and connecting with each brain. Get an inner sense of how each brain feels to you. Return your hand to your heart and take a deep breath to calm yourself and formulate your question.

2. When you ask your question, you'll place your hand on one brain, ask the question, and wait for an answer. Then you'll place your hand on the next brain, and the next, while asking each brain the same question.

3. Ask a question. Start with a simple question that requires a yes or no response. We know you want to jump in with big questions, but trust us. Don't take an emotionally-laden topic and expect your head, heart, and gut to go into therapy discussions with you. Just ask a simple question, see how HUG responds, feel the truth of the responses, and learn to trust it. Trust is only established through repeating a successful experience. See what happens next because when knowledge rises to the surface, you will see situations or people differently. There may be one answer. There may be three answers, which require you to ask again, dig deeper, and learn to read how your head, heart and gut respond to you.

    For example, if you are a risk-taker who jumps into life without thinking about consequences, your head brain will say, "Sure, jump in that pool. Go for it." And your gut may be practical and say, "Check for water in the pool before you jump, okay?"

4. How do you receive the answer? Do you hear it inside? Do you get an image? Can you feel it? Write down your impressions. Write down your awareness.

5. Warning! We suggest people start with their heart or gut first, and then move to the next brain, and ask the head brain last. The majority of people live in their head, so best to start somewhere else, otherwise you might find it hard to leave the safe place of your head and get another opinion.

6. Another way to bypass the head or get started with the heart is to imagine that you get on an elevator and push the down button. See the elevator stop at the heart and visualize yourself sitting in the center of your heart. Place your hand on your heart and ask your question. If you say, "I think I have it," you don't because *think* comes from the head. You might have unknowingly let the elevator rise back up the throat and return to where it feels safe. Ride the elevator again until you are back in your heart.

7. If you find that you choose not to go to the heart or you are afraid of being too vulnerable, then don't force the issue. We respect the heart's right to feel safe, and you will want to learn to trust your heart again through coaching, spiritual counseling, or therapy. Simply dialogue between your gut and head for a while and then ask the heart when it will be ready.

Examples

In the sample outline in the chart on page 61, Caron guided Victoria—who wanted to drink her morning coffee after her doctor told her she shouldn't drink coffee—how to ask an honest question the right way. In Victoria's first response to the question CAN I drink it, the answer was obvious. Of course she can, but that wasn't what she wanted to know. Her three brains responded honestly and reflected the part of her that tells her to go ahead and let's her know the result in the gut.

In the second question, she asked if her body benefitted in any healthy way from drinking coffee. She was not happy with the response, but she was happy that she could finally tune in to her inner wisdom to guide healthy life temperament choices. She chose a chai tea to drink while watching the sunrise.

Samples

First Example: Victoria

Question	Head Logic-Reason	Heart Emotional Center	Gut Intuitive-practical
Can my body drink my morning coffee?	You shouldn't with your current meds.	Yes, you enjoy it. Have one morning cup of java.	Only if you wish to continue to irritate your colon.
Is drinking one cup of morning coffee beneficial to my health?	No	It is not the coffee you enjoy while watching the sunrise. You enjoy the sunrise, and you'll still enjoy it without coffee.	Only if you wish to irritate the colon.

Second Example: Susan

In this second example, Susan is struggling to make a decision about sending her son to preschool in the fall. See how she uses HUG to work through her feelings. Susan is a visual learner, so we had her draw a chart and write out her answers on a piece of paper in a more representative format. Choose which style works best for your temperament. See example on page 62.

It can also be helpful to do the HUG technique with a partner who can write while you talk, freeing you to focus on listening.

Goal: Clarify whether my two-year-old Eric is ready for preschool or does he need to stay home one more year.

Questions for HUG: Is Eric ready for preschool? Is it in Eric's higher good to be at home one more year?

Question	Head Logic-Reason	Heart Emotional Center	Gut Intuitive-practical
Is Eric ready for preschool?	Yes, ready to specialize with new friends and have structured play-time.	No, you feel he is too young, and question whether he would get more than you already give him.	Yes, he is ready and you are ready.
Is it in Eric's higher good to be at home one more year?	Eric is fine at home or at school. Both serve his highest good.	Yes, preschool serves his highest good.	Eric will be fine at home or school. You can choose the best for both of you now.

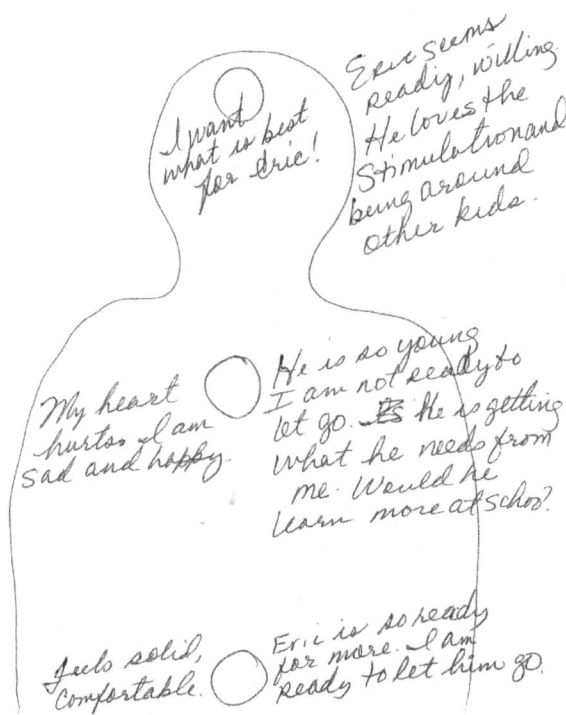

I want what is best for Eric!

Eric seems ready, willing. He loves the stimulation and being around other kids.

My heart hurts. I am sad and happy.

He is so young. I am not ready to let go. Is he getting what he needs from me. Would he learn more at school?

Feels solid, comfortable.

Eric is so ready for more. I am ready to let him go.

Now, it's Your Turn to Practice

1. Formulate your questions.

2. Place your hand on one of the three brains.

3. Write down your answer on the corresponding spot on the outline or draw a figure like Susan's on a piece of paper.

4. Repeat with other two segments on the chart.

5. If your answers agree with each other, trust them and take action.

6. If your actions do not agree with each other, then ask each voice why. Clarify, ask questions differently, or ask what you should know or understand right now.

Record your practice with HUG™ here.

Question	Head Logic-Reason	Heart Emotional Center	Gut Intuitive-practical
1.			
2.			

Chapter Five

Tool Four Is Stopping Emotional Hijacking

Thus far, you have learned that three topics can be the cause of issues or disconnection in relationships:

1. The core temperament that you were born with predisposes you to certain tendencies and preferences in how you learn, respond to stress, like or dislike people, and your ability to communicate with others. Much of the communication breakdown you have with other people may result from hard-wired predispositions built in during your childhood.

2. Likewise, sets of values clash in a relationship, causing one to show lack of respect for the values of the other. You cannot expect another person to know what it is that you value: perhaps you never told them. Perhaps you are the one to model and explain values to help a colleague or child learn how to discern their best choices.

3. Your choice of an intimate partner and the quality of your relationships with others are affected by memories of your early parent–child bond. Your fun with children and sizzle with a friend or partner fizzle when **an emotional memory hijacks your awareness** and you respond as you did when you were 4 or 8 or 12 or 16 or 25.

Emotional hijacking means that patterns burned into your brain as a child or teen - any trauma really - raise that primitive alarm system and your nervous system screams: "Run, stop, freeze, hit, yell!" When you are having a normal conversation, a tone of voice, facial response, or movement can cause your natural instincts to react without conscious thought. When a child is tired and throws a tantrum, one parent responds with love and attention and becomes concerned about low blood sugar levels. Another parent becomes embarrassed that people think he's a bad parent and threatens the child, which actually makes his greatest fear come true. Everyone will look at that parent and think, "Poor child, bad parent." Which parent is responding through emotional hijacking? Yes, the second one.

Hijacking makes you respond in the stress response pattern of your temperament: get angry; withdraw and worry; laugh it off and escape; feel unappreciated, disrespected, abandoned, or made fun of; or shrink inside. Instead of having the ability to be present with people today, you are worrying or feeling flooded with strong emotions from yesteryear.

Love That Hijacking!

Emotional hijacking means that you respond from the survival patterns developed earlier in life. Of course, you are an adult now, and everyone says you should be responsible and have your emotions in check...Ha! Believe us, those people who seem to have it all together worked hard and consistently to get there - because they reached a point of being tired of the patterns, the pain, and the problems that resulted from always feeling scared, threatened, abandoned, pressured, and so on.

Once you get there, something magical happens: you get really tired of the trauma and the drama and want something more—something better, freer, gentler, more peaceful, safer, kinder, and more caring. You realize that you deserve better: then you seek how to be better and learn what you have to do. You go for the gold; learning to accept, forgive, integrate, and enjoy.

So why do we love hijacking? Because you wouldn't be here without it. Your child-self learned how to be resilient and you survived, right? You have that hijacking habit of yours to thank. Let us celebrate with you that you survived to be the person you are today and share your strength with the world. Reading this book will continue to guide you, shedding more light on those hijackings and making use of this awareness to be in the best relationships ever. For example,

Liz's dad died in the first Gulf War when she was eight years old, and she has realized that her neediness hijacks her ability to relax and go with the flow in any dating relationship. Instead she is habitually nervous and afraid she'll do something wrong.

As she learned to relax, she has changed her emotional behavior. If she perceives disrespect, she's learned to take ownership of her perception and her reaction to it. Her date is not being disrespectful when he speaks about his first love or the wife who recently died of breast cancer. He is not abandoning Liz: he is just telling his story, which triggers her own memories of loss and why she used to react like she was eight again. Liz has learned to say to herself, "This is not about me." Her new reaction is to empathize with her date's loss and let him know she understands and has had a similar experience. Through the loss of her father, Liz has gained great empathy for others who have lost someone. That r esilience is her strength: she uses it to escape from the assumption that her companion didn't respect her when he spoke of his own loss.

Instead of running away from her fear of loss, she can be present with her date and witness his story. She has shown maturity in her emotional development by empathizing. Her date now sees that she

genuinely cares for about him. Her eyes no longer wander, avoiding his eyes and giving him the idea that she lacks interest in him and in his story.

How did Liz learn to notice her hijacking patterns and start to make changes? She learned to name them, watch out for them and then tame them by changing her responses to them. Liz told us that she could tell when her memories started to take over. First she noticed that her body felt tense and a little anxious. Negative thoughts arose: "Why is he telling me about his first love? Who cares? Isn't he enjoying the evening?" In other words, in her mind she left the elegant dining room, stopped listening to a grieving friend and started worrying. She has now learned to set her negative thoughts aside, and shift back to the dining room to listen to her friend.

How to Dig Deeper

Using the chart on page 67 see whether you recognize any patterns from core temperaments that resemble your own behavior patterns brought on by emotional hijacking.

Instructions:

1. Read the statement in the left column and describe similar responses of your own. Read all of the statements as you may find you have reactions from any or all of the four core temperaments, even if it is not your primary temperament.

2. For each reaction you list, dig deeper and explore and all the emotional memories that surface when you are triggered by this particular reaction.

3. Suggestion for HUG question. Ask yourself: What is the best way for me to change or manage this emotional reaction right NOW? Record your response.

4. List the resilience skills you have learned or want to learn from this experience.

Lisa is a 52 year old schoolteacher and a single mother of twelve-year old twin boys. She is struggling with her professional relationship with the principal of the elementary school where she teaches fifth grade.

Lisa has a combination of core temperaments: she is a Detective as well as a Border Collie. The principal meets with each teacher once a week to determine lesson plans, supplies to order, and respond to any administrative issues. Lisa notes her responses to him fall into two types.

Her Detective temperament gets irritated at what she perceives as his condescending attitude. Lisa feels impatient when she perceives he is just going on and on. Then like a Border Collie, the longer he talks, the more she withdraws from the conversation, and her thoughts turn to self-criticism: why is he reviewing classroom discipline? Did a parent complain? Does he want to fire me because I am older?

Digging Deeper: Explore your Responses to Emotional Memories

Bulldozer	Your Response	Emotional Memory	HUG response	Skill Learned
Tries harder to do something about it				
Stops talking purposefully				
Withdraws				
Loses temper				
Gets angry or aggressive				
Detective				
Starts nitpicking				
Becomes preoccupied with thoughts				
Worries or blames				
Sulks				
Becomes irritated and impatient				
Border Collie				
Withdraws from violence, loudness, or anger				
Becomes moody				
Feels depressed				
Suffers in silence				
Criticizes self				
Stops talking about it or to you				
Ringmaster				
Talks at you, as if to convince you				
Uses humor to lighten the load or turns the humor on you				
Wants to escape, looks for a way out				
Indulges an addiction like spending, eating, or drinking				
Changes mind, breaks a promise				
Goes to someone else for advice or empathy				
Simply leaves				

Note: you can print this and many of the other forms in this book at http://www.heartwiserelationships.com.

See how Lisa used the chart to work through her habitual responses to her boss and come up with a new course of action.

Detective

Lisa's Response: I start to worry about him talking so long, I wonder if there is more to it, I feel paranoid and worried about my job.

Emotional Memory: My mom divorced my Dad and used to go on and on about my father and how hard being a single mom was. I tuned her out as a kid. I wondered why she told me "adult stuff." The pattern made me worry for her.

HUG response: I need to trust I am safe and doing my job well. It is okay to speak up and interrupt him. Or I could set a time limit for the meeting. Be proactive, not passive just because he is an authority figure.

Skill Learned : As a child, I learned to be too passive. My resilience skill to practice is speaking up and setting boundaries.

Add this information to your core temperament profile so you can keep the various parts of your exploration and assessment together so you can continue to reveal and understand who you are, and, thereby, who you can *be* in relationships. The next section will help you understand how emotional memories are formed and how you developed your own emotional reactions. This knowledge answers the big question: "Why am I the way I am?"

Knowledge is power: the more you understand yourself and those in relationships with you, the easier it is to make repairs from compassion and the desire for that sizzle that love offers.

Relational Intimacy = Ability to Be Aware or Present

Your maturity, emotional growth, and ability to have intimate friendships and relationships throughout life evolve as your core temperament adapts to people and experiences. This shapes your core temperament. The goal of repairing relationships is to learn how to be in relationship without emotional hijacking: it is real, it is possible, and it is marvelous. The result is intimacy—that depth in a friendship, partnership, or parenthood that feeds your heart and soul.

Intimacy does not exist apart from your individual development. Interpersonal interactions and relationships modify the ways you respond and how you cope. The goal is integrating intimacy into all aspects of your life. This is the true meaning of "no man is an island." You are hard-wired for relationships.

"The opposite of Loneliness is not Togetherness, it's Intimacy"
~ Richard Bach

Let's review the early parent-child bond so you understand how your choice of an intimate partner and the quality of your relationships is defined by memories of your early parent–child bond. If some of your earlier memories are of trauma or terror, you can seek professional help since the hijacking of *you* may be beyond your control. Maybe you did not have a happy childhood. Who did? Does it matter? Your task—as you move to intimate relationships with depth and commitment—is learning how to manage your hijacking episodes, both for your own good and for the good of those you love.

Intimacy Is the Goal from Birth

New insights into brain development clarify what it takes to develop productive relationships and maintain them at home and at work. Studies show why vast numbers of people have great difficulty communicating with the most important people in their work and love lives. What does it take to *build and nurture* productive, meaningful, life-long relationships?

The basis of meaningful or intimate relationships is secure infant/adult interactions that result in a successful, *secure* bonding. A mother, father, nanny, or other primary caregiver senses a babe's feelings, needs, and emotions. This triggers in child and caretaker an empathy hormone called oxytocin, which the mother produces through soothing touch, nursing, voice, eye gazing, and stroking of her child. Yet, whichever empathic adult is responding to the infant, the child and parent sense the other's feelings and emotions at the visceral level. A baby cries, a mother's womb wrenches in response, urging her to care for the babe. A toddler falls and reaches up, a father's smile and caring hands cuddle the child to his chest, where the heartbeat reassures with a feeling of safety and love. In other words, an infant feels safe and understood when the caregiver responds to cries and accurately interprets and is responsive to her needs.*

This need for empathy and kindness continues throughout your entire life, no matter how much of a lone wolf you declare yourself to be or how hurt you feel.

The Foundation of Intimacy is Bonding through Responsiveness

An adult continues to need empathy, responsiveness, touch, and caring like the human infant needs them: they are basic human needs. A caretaker is emotionally available to a baby or toddler or

---

*For more information about Parenting Responsively see the Relationship Resources page at the end of this book.

youngster, beyond just meeting his physical needs. As the child responds and adapts to emotionally available people in his or her early years, so he develops empathy and learns to be responsive in return. Responsiveness is a two-way street.

Not having an empathic or responsive adult in the early years could well be the reason that a child - or adult - is crushed and deeply hurt, even feeling abandoned, when a parent isolates the child or an intimate withdraws from conversation and punishes the partner with silence or emotional isolation. Such relations stem from early distancing or trauma and often hijacks us as adults, showing up as fear and adverse reactions - which are our basic defense mechanisms.

The development of such defenses can start with trauma at any point in your life. However, there are windows during which you are especially vulnerable to the activation of this process. The blueprint for relationships in your life is strongly shaped by the level of trust and acceptance you experienced early on. Early in life, you are exquisitely sensitive to the emotional atmosphere of your home and the messages from your caregivers. Their messages have told you, in words or no words, which behaviors and traits are desirable.

Successful bonding in conjunction with your core temperament sets up your relationship blueprint: how you, as an adult

- Respond to stress
- Empathize with another person
- Use body language and facial expressions to communicate
- Are able to mutually engage
- Are able to forgive

As an adult, you still have basic human or ego needs that affect your relationships. You'll recognize needs in two types:

1. Your **inner needs** are driven by your core temperaments and your values. As a Bulldozer, you may feel the need to earn money, compete, stay busy, or focus on a special new project. As a Detective, you need to learn new materials, teach what you know, and keep your logical mind focused on curiosity and discovery, or you become bored. As a Border Collie, you have a need to serve, to be appreciated and cared for. You desire to fulfill your heart by helping others. As a Ringmaster, your need to thrive on admiration for your creative works and accomplishments is genuine: if a song plays in your head or an inner wisdom desires expression, you express it. Your ability to network and influence others for the better motivates everything you do.

2. Your **external needs** relate to personal reputation, status, recognition, appreciation and the respect of family and friends. These are motivated by your environment and relationships.

How your needs were met as a child influence how you meet your needs today. Have no judgments or beliefs about either internal or external demonstration of needs: they are what they are, one not being better or preferred over the other. This knowledge serves you in knowing how to raise kids and how to respond to adults in relationships, especially if you observe defensive behaviors or hijacking by your own emotional memories. Always decode such behaviors by asking yourself what this person in your relationship needs right now. Once you decode a partner's or child's need, you can either provide that need or show those in relationship with you how to meet their needs themselves.

Defensive Behaviors

Your **defense mechanisms** are subconscious, almost automatic reactions that protect you from unpleasant situations. People use these defenses to soften feelings of failure, to alleviate feelings of guilt, and to protect their sense of personal worth or adequacy. Everyone has defense mechanisms and we don't judge them. Each of us has survived defensive tactics like emotional hijackings that interfere with good relationships. Are you here reading? Then your defensive tactics worked!

The way to deal with a defensive behavior is first to see what yours are, then see if they get in the way of loving as deeply as you want to love or if they cause you to push people away who want to love you.

Here is a serious thought for you to consider: sometimes you may be the most defensive with someone whom you really love because you finally feel safe enough with them to be your real self. Be careful how you act out; you can say "No" to pushing this wonderful person away. On the other hand, if your gut, heart, and other body parts start rattling and being defensive because you **do not feel safe**, then listen to your body. Seek help, conversation, or counseling to discern if you are escaping because the danger is real or because love is close. If you cannot tell the difference, then your emotional hijacking is real, and you are not ready to make choices about it by yourself. Seek help or support to discern your defensive patterns and how they are affecting your relationships. The following chart will help you decide which hijacking patterns disrupt your relationships the most.

Defensive Consequences Worksheet

Use the Defensive Behaviors worksheet on the page 73-74 to look at your personal defensive behaviors. Remember: when you name it, you can tame it. Understanding this piece of the relationship puzzle will immediately move you from fizzle to sizzle: it is a core reason why it takes just one person to implement change.

Gloria is a Border Collie who sees the world through rose-colored glasses. She chooses to always see the best in other people. Unfortunately, her rosy outlook hasn't always served her well in relationships. As a 30-year-old single nurse, Gloria wanted to be in a loving marriage. During her dating years, she rationalized the faults and shortcomings of each of her dates. She focused so hard on what was right about each one that she failed to see that their values clashed or their personal temperaments were completely incompatible with hers. She habitually avoided the discomfort of getting too close to them or letting them get too close to her. She avoided confronting a date when he didn't return her call or explain why he didn't want to see her again; she just said, "Oh, he must be busy," or "I guess I am just not the right person for him."

Finally Gloria recognized that she was rationalizing other people's reactions to her and she learned to identify the emotional trigger from her childhood. Her father had abandoned her and her mother when Gloria was only two. Her mother constantly warned her about getting too close to men because they would leave her. Her own discomfort and fear caused her to absorb the blame for her failed relationships rather than see that perhaps the truth was very simple or had nothing to do with her at all. Once Gloria realized that she was making excuses and trying too hard to see people in their best light, she was able to start acknowledging her fears of abandonment and intimacy and to empathize with others who shared that fear. She eventually found a partner she loved deeply. Together they were able to work through their mutual fears of intimacy and achieve a rewarding relationship based on trust and unconditional love.

Defensive Behaviors Worksheet

Types of Defensive Behaviors	Long Term Discomfort I am Avoiding	Short Term Defensive Strategy	Consequences
Compensation = **defensive behavior that offsets, excuses, or hides a weakness**			
You might use compensation to disguise the presence of a weak or undesirable quality by emphasizing a more positive one. For example, you may think you are not attractive and buy expensive clothes to look better. You may feel uncomfortable around a large group of people at a party and talk too loud and crack jokes to try to fit in.			
Projection - **unconscious projection of personal feelings or representation**			
You might use projection by assigning blame for your own mistakes or shortcomings to someone else. You attribute motives and desires also to other people, as if seeing in them what you are experiencing in that moment: for example you might be afraid to hear a medical diagnosis and assume the doctor is scared to tell you about it.			
Rationalization – **making something seem more attractive, justifying, excusing**			
You offer excuses for behavior instead of telling the real reason. You justify actions that are unacceptable to you or to how you are perceived by others, often to save face. Rationalization is an attempt to make situations more plausible.			
Denial of Reality – **refusing to accept or acknowledge inconvenient truths**			
You may ignore or refuse to acknowledge disagreeable realities. You may turn away from unpleasant situations or stress overloads, refuse to discuss unpopular topics, or reject criticism rather than deal with them.			

***Reaction formation* – a protection by telling one-self the opposite truths**			
You use reaction formation to hide from your deeper truths. You tell yourself you don't care what people think when you really do and in fact worry about it. You choose not to be in relationship by telling yourself you like being alone and don't have time for other people - when your deeper truth is that you want to be loved.			
***Flight* – need to escape, flee from the perceived danger, not face the trauma, the fear, or the emotional trigger**			
You escape from frustrating situations by taking flight, physically or mentally. To take flight physically, you develop symptoms or ailments that provide excuses for removing yourself from difficult or frustrating situations.			
You escape mentally by daydreaming or withdraw from achieving a task or your goals in recognition of some deeper anxiety or worry. If you react in an extreme way, begin to confuse fantasy with reality.			
***Aggression* – behavior that is forceful, vindictive, and hostile**			
You use aggression when you experience the normal human emotion of anger. When you do not control or manage anger, you become hostile and direct your antagonism or belligerence at a person or an object. Aggression intends to harm.			
Resignation			
You use resignation as a sign of giving up after frustration, anxiety, trying too hard, or not feeling listened to, appreciated or respected. Resignation means putting less energy than is called for into an effort or relationship or discussion. For some people, it is a calm acceptance; for others, resignation is giving up. Which is it for you?			

Being Aware Means Being the Change You Want to See

"Be the change you want to see in the world." - Mahatma Gandhi

When you see yourself consistently reacting in one of these defensive postures, you will have an "Ah-ha!" realization. You named it, and you can tame it!

Being aware of defensive reactions means you finally understand that the repetitive reaction, the hijacking in the present moment, is an ineffective way to get your needs met. Now you can plan your relationships to meet your needs, developing a new "relationship blueprint." Gradually, as you notice or are able, you are creating a reliable response and implementing it with **someone you trust.** The best new response in a relationship is one that comes from your own alignment of head, heart, and gut, because you will be following your truth and values. Trying to be any other way in relationship just doesn't work.

What Do Bonding and Intimacy Look Like In Adulthood?

A reader, Leon, asked us this question: "So, look, Dr. Goode and Dr. Riordan, I understand all that birth and baby bonding stuff, and my childhood was far from perfect. How does knowing any of this help me save my marriage, communicate with my teenager, encourage my involvement in my management team, or have an enjoyable date night with my spouse?"

Our answer is that each core temperament has a tendency to follow specific emotional patterns, and these are enhanced, triggered, or shaped when you are a baby and child. These patterns are not set in concrete, though: recent scientific work has shown that the human brain continues to adapt throughout your adult years. Habits are not fixed - they can be changed - and we would be remiss if we failed to mention that making the changes requires your willingness, readiness, commitment, and consistency. Otherwise, you truly will be like a hamster in a wheel, running in circles and wondering why you aren't making any progress.

As a human being, you are capable of adapting to your environment and gaining new skills: that's resilience. As an adult, you accept who you are, keep the good from your past, and move on or change what is not working. For example,

- Babies cry because their bodies send feeling signals to the brain. They do not rationalize it. Your first clue as an adult is to recognize and name the feelings in your body. Pay attention and quit ignoring or denying feelings or rationalizing them. **Name it and tame it.**

- Babies feel safe when their caregivers demonstrate empathy for their feelings and respond respectfully. Magical as well as chemical bonding happens when that empathy gene kicks in. Thus, your second clue as an adult is to **be tuned in to each other's feelings, and have the capacity to communicate them constructively.**

- And, Leon, the tool is **the ability to respond appropriately** to your intimate, friend, colleague, or child. Being responsive in an emotionally intelligent way includes listening and observing body language, accepting what is said without judgement or negative comments, being supportive, determining if you can help, or modeling appropriate behavior for a child.

Think actions and words that reflect kindness, compassion, and respect space and boundaries.

You are a marvelously resilient being with a unique core temperament. You develop habits from whatever kind of bonding you received. You CAN change your reactions into responses.

So Leon, the next time your wife spends the entire evening complaining about your relationship while you are on a dinner date, try not to respond defensively. We also recommend telling her what your expectations are for the romantic evening ahead of time: create the evening you want.

When we can recognize knee-jerk memories, expectations, attitudes, assumptions and behaviors as problems resulting from insecure attachment bonds, we can end their influence on our adult relationships. That recognition allows us to reconstruct the healthy nonverbal communication skills that produce an attuned attachment and successful relationships. ~ Jeanne Segal, Ph.D., Jaelline Jaffe, Ph.D., and Suzanne Barston

Science tells us that it takes 21 days for the biochemistry of old patterns to start changing and within six months a human being can adapt to almost any situation. As authors, we help people celebrate transitions because we know that in six months, they can adapt and be very happy. But you have to be willing to change habits and to work at breaking old patterns. None of us is perfect, but if what we want the most from our relationships is intimacy and happiness, then following the steps for relationship repair in this book will set you on the right road to transformation.

The next time Leon invited his wife to dinner, he explained his hopes and expectations for an evening out. He told her how much it hurt his feelings to sit through a dinner of her complaining about what was wrong in their lives rather than focusing on the joy of an evening together. They agreed to set aside quiet time at home to discuss what was and wasn't working in their relationship before they went out. Once they both created the opportunity to fully listen and accept how each was feeling, they were able to enjoy their date night for what it was: a romantic evening without the kids.

Any change of behavior results from action. You have to implement both physical and mental activity for your body to say, "Oh this is new! We like this." You can feel, be aware of how you react, and choose to be willing and ready to adapt again when you desire intimacy and friendship, or when your child needs a new behavioral model to adapt.

Our steps for relationship repair help you gauge how willing you are to change by noticing your behaviors and catching yourself when you tend to react, blow up or respond with anger, withdrawal, ridicule or judgment. We ask that you commit to 21 days of practice noticing your behaviors without judging them.

We remind you that it only takes one person in a relationship to make a difference. Do not expect the other person to change without your invitation. You can only control your own responses: commit to repairing yourself first.

Intimacy--How You Progress Through Love and Lust Throughout Life

> *The first step toward change is acceptance. Once you accept yourself, you open the door to change. That's all you have to do. Change is not something you do, it's something you allow.*
> ~Will Garcia

Intimacy starts with familiarity, trust, and tenderness, and grows into affection and closeness. Intimacy has dimensions that you experience every day with different people: closeness, conversation, hugs, a shared space or atmosphere that grows into mutual privacy and intimate knowledge of how people behave in their own skin, so to speak.

As humans with the same physical and emotional equipment as well as relationship opportunities, we dance with lust and love throughout each decade of our lives. Socially, as humans, we must achieve certain cognitive and emotional goals to handle relationships well.

What if we don't manage to be successful in our developmental goals in our 20s, 30s, 40s, 50s, or 60s? Then we adapt and learn or we don't always have successful relationships. Let's take a look at how you grew up and developed relationship skills.

Your Early Adulthood

Just as young people mature physically, they also mature socially, developing their thinking and learning abilities. Although you may not realize it, as you progressed from adolescence to young adulthood and then on to middle adulthood, significant changes occurred in the way you thought and viewed the world: changes which influenced your ability to experience intimacy.

In your teen years, your thinking was dualistic and you viewed people and events as good or bad, black or white, right or wrong. This changes in later years to understanding and allowing each person to have the right to their opinion. (*That's your opinion and you're entitled to it. You can believe that, but I don't have to.*) Next comes the questioning of authority and the understanding that those in authority don't have all the answers. (*I'm not sure what you are telling me is true. How do you know that? I read a book that tells me otherwise. My professor doesn't agree with you. How do I know you are right? Prove it.*)

How you think or thought about people in your late teens either means you are judgmental (black or white), more circumspect, or open to new ideas. Higher levels of flexibility and openness make establishing relationships easier. Greater rigidity or inflexible thinking, such as the need to be right or perfect, diminishes the ease in your relationships—unless your best friend is your dog that loves you unconditionally and can't fight back.

Most young adults mature into completely recognizing the idea that truth is relative, and knowledge is constructed and not absolute. This presents itself as the allowance and acceptance of the opinions of others. When you can allow other people their opinions or knowledge, you have reached a high level of self-esteem and comfort with your self.

If as an adult, you take someone's words or ideas personally through a negative emotional reaction, you might be experiencing a clash of values, or reliving emotional damage from your tender years as a thinking teen.

- When this happens, review your values list to determine if you felt defensive about one of your values.

- Stop and think about your views of people. What level of understanding have you reached: dualistic, relative, accepting, judgmental? Knowing where you are is important because your communication with people is based on your level of understanding.

- If you recognize other people's levels of thinking, it will allow you to communicate clearly. Clear communication is at the center of understanding temperament and repairing relationships.

Today's young adults are in a new stage of life, called emerging adulthood, which extends from late teens into the twenties and is defined by today's changing cultural, social and financial pressures. Emerging adulthood implies that stepping into adult roles is delayed, but the transition time is spent exploring new roles, experiencing the depth and breadth of knowledge, taking time to travel the world, and exploring interests such as politics, the environment, or differing cultures.

Erik Erikson developed his theory[1] that a person's identity formation (i.e. knowing one's self and developing the self-image) grows and expands throughout one's lifetime by accomplishing certain tasks at each age. In Erikson's model, Relationship Skill Development means exploring one's ability to relate intimately to another human being. While personal identity formation develops from late teens throughout your twenties and beyond, those who do not develop healthy relationship skills have further difficulties, such as feeling isolated and alone as they mature. The development process looks like this:

1. Teens need to develop an internal self-image or persona. This personal identity includes their core temperament, their values, and relational skills. Success in forming a personal identity means an ability to stay true to yourself, while failure leads to role confusion and a weak self-image.

2. In the teen years, relationships are about falling in and out of lust and love, and exploring romance, friendships, and varied levels of intimacy: tenderness, concern, kindness, desire for reciprocity of affections and caring.

3. Love means knowing someone at a deeper level than friendship, feeling connected and familiar.

4. Sexual relationships may be explored as part of the longing to know another, but they don't usually imply commitment.

5. Intimacy with another is achieved when both people in a relationship feel close and have such mutual satisfaction that each can make a personal commitment, according to Erickson's theory.

Justin met Traci at a freshman mixer in the first month of college. In sharing their stories, they discovered that each was raised by a single parent and each had experienced feelings of loss and abandonment in the absence of the second parent. They clicked instantly and began the dating ritual. Both were smart students and carried a heavier than normal class load, which required focused study. They often did this together, then had sex, shared meals, took long walks or had a movie night. Like sponges, they absorbed each other and explored intimacy in varied ways—discussions, debates, touching, studying, and practicing for exams. They moved in together after completion of their freshman year: they felt

---

[1] To learn more about Erikson's theory visit: http://www.education.com/reference/article/identity-development/

they didn't need anyone else, since their love was complete.

They were in love and planned to be married after college. But their perceptions changed after a campus fraternity invited Justin to pledge during his sophomore year. Justin was flattered and felt caught between his love for Traci and his desire to find out if he could really make it into a prestigious fraternity. Traci could feel him gradually pull away as he accepted the pledge invitation. Traci found herself alone in their apartment. She didn't like the changes in Justin's personality that resulted from drinking with the fraternity brothers.

She grew more silent and withdrew. He blamed her and drank more. With a tender heart and many tears, Traci knew she had to break away from Justin or get sucked into his drama and lose her sense of self. Her values were to continue her education through to her PhD and then move into a career as a medical researcher. She had already received offers because of her brilliance. Jason used to share her vision for their future and supported her; they believed love would last forever and weather any bad storms.

Traci learned a hard lesson and missed him terribly for that whole year of school, but changed schools for her junior year so she could better pursue what she needed to do. Justin partied two more years, and then the school put all members of his fraternity on probation for some harsh pranks. He lost his high grade point average. He called Traci and pursued her for the next two years, but she waited until he could understand his contribution to their break up - he finally owned up to it but was still angry. After her first love, Traci moved on and did manage to articulate and form her identity after her first love. Despite her love for him she stuck to her value and chose not to pursue a relationship with someone who had addiction problems. Justin still had growing up to do to understand his role in the relationship and to be able to form a self-image separate from Traci within their relationship.

Young adults learn to balance their individual needs for independence, career interests, and friends with the need for the emotional and sexual intimacy found in a close relationship.

Isolation occurs, as it did for Justin, when the young adult is unable to establish a committed relationship with a partner. As mentioned previously, causes can be disappointments, unresolved bonding and trust issues, or low self-esteem. Adults who have not achieved this level of development may seek out superficial relationships and/or focus on career or social projects in lieu of pursuing intimacy.

Questions for Review

In looking at how young adults develop in relationships, ask yourself what you were like as a young adult:

- How did you conduct yourself in relationships?

- When was your first serious romantic involvement?

- How did it end?

- What did you learn from the experience?

- Do you struggle with intimacy today and can you see now what the root causes of your struggle are?

- During the teen years, how did you respond to hurt, disappointment, loss, and failed expectations?

We encourage you to keep a journal of your experiences as you gain insight and a deeper understanding of your personal relationship milestones. A helpful way to do that is to create a time line of your relationship history, like Mary's partial history shown below.

Doing this activity shows that how you are reacting now is tempered by prior relational experience; it may also help you to understand why you avoid intimacy, commitment and love.

Mary's Relationship Time line

1982 – First boyfriend at age 13, young love, fun, not serious, I remember him fondly, Michael. He gave me a friendship ring with two hearts on it.

1983 – 1987 High school years, a few dates but no serious boyfriends. I don't understand why boys call once or twice and then just stop calling. What did I do wrong? Is it okay for me to call them? Why aren't they interested in me?

1987 – 1990 I was raped at the end of my freshman year in college. Never had a lot of relationships, no sex, a few dates, but no one serious after that. Kept myself emotionally distant from everyone, and didn't tell anyone about what had happened.

1990 – 1993 Party years! Went on the pill, had lots of sexual activity, no one serious until Matt came along. I felt like he was the first person who really saw me! I was so in love, and then he broke my heart by dating someone else without even telling me.

2000 – Got married to Mitch. He's easy to be with. I know he loves me, but after ten years, it seems like we should be happier. Something is not working. He wants more from me than I give.

You can see from Mary's experience why she struggles with intimacy and how she feels the need to protect herself.

Mary was always successful academically and got a great job after college, but success in her outer world did not mean she could be emotionally available to another person intimately. As her career advanced, her creative talents and leadership abilities were recognized, and she took on more and more responsibility at work. Mary began working with Dr. Goode when her marriage was on the rocks. Mary did not want a divorce: she loved her husband, but she felt overwhelmed by his neediness. Mary learned that her core temperament is the Bulldozer, tempered by the Border Collie. She likes to achieve and feels fulfilled when she completes her professional goal - yet she can also be supportive of Mitch if she commits to that.

Her husband Mitch is predominantly a Border Collie temperament, but the Detective temperament follows a close second. He is careful with their finances, and is great at completing those "honey-do" lists. He wants more emotional intimacy with Mary and to recapture the romance of their early years before they had kids and before Mary's promotion, but he doesn't know how to communicate that to Mary.

When the two finally understood their personal histories, core temperaments and conflicting values, Mary was able to see how her past history and need for security and distance were driving Mitch away. Together they were able to create a vision for their romantic relationship and their life together.

Mary made an effort for Mitch with romantic dinners, walks and alone time. She also learned to check in with her head, heart, and gut before responding to a difficult conversation with him. She shared what happened to her in college for the first time and Mitch is supporting her as she comes to terms with this experience, while learning about himself, too. By using the four tools laid out in this book, Mary and Mitch are ready to tackle their relationship challenges going forward.

Like most young adults nowadays, as you enter the decade of your 20s and leave childhood behind, you have become more in charge of your life and in control of your choices. At the same time you have been exploring, learning, and trying on new roles as you transitioned to adulthood.

Questions for Review

If you do not feel in charge of your life, answer these questions and add to your profile as questions to address with HUG:

1. In what area of your life do you not feel in control?
2. What are your emotional responses to not feeling in control? Please take note of this now so you can compare your emotional skills to the chart of core emotional predispositions.

Your 30s

Continuing from young adult tasks into your 30s involves laying the groundwork for and establishing your personal identity and behavior in love and at work.

As you transition from your 20s and 30s you spend a lot of time weaving these parts of life together. Young adults plan and change course more often than any other age group. When their decisions are aligned with their self-view, values and the social worlds they live in, they acquire competence in several areas, and life begins to become full and rewarding. Here is what is happening in your 30s:

1. You apply your intelligence and insight to reach for goals involving career, education, relationships, and having children.

2. These choices have profound consequences for you, the maturing adult. Why? Because at this stage in life, others assume you have developed the self-awareness to monitor and adapt your behavior, especially in relationships with other people. The truth is, your adolescent brain may just be catching up with your roles in life. For example, some young adults don't know what they want to do with their lives professionally until they reach their thirties; others are just starting to manage their emotional impulses in a more mature manner.

3. At this stage responsibilities include attention and time for spouse and children. Social responsibilities increase for people in work situations, and career planning. There is also responsibility to your larger community, perhaps in volunteering, sports involvement, and parental care.

4. In your thirties, you face multiple truths and have to find your place and define your own reality. Do you have initiative and feel confident enough to go after life - or do you feel guilty or naïve as a follower? Do you believe you are not matching up to your own expectations of self? Are others' expectations of you right on or too high? In this decade you are expected to accept responsibility for your actions rather than blaming others. Sometimes it feels like you must grow up or seek a lifestyle that suits your reality and personal truth outside the mainstream, as many Ringmasters do. They are excellent entrepreneurs.

Questions for Review

If you are in your thirties, review how well you are achieving your milestones in the emotional sense. If you are in later decades, assess what your relationships were like during your 30s:

- Do you know your values as an individual?

- Do you know you partner's values and understand his or her viewpoint?

- On a scale of 1-10 with 1 being *Very Dissatisfied* and 10 being *Very Satisfied*, how do you like your current intimate relationship?

- Explain your score.

- Do you take the initiative to solve problems and make changes?

40s & 50s = Midlife

In Midlife your outcomes manifest themselves as less practicality-driven and more creative. Erikson tagged the challenge of these decades as not becoming self-absorbed: your strengths of these decades are self-care and staying productive. Review this list and determine if you have achieved the goals of self-identification and dealing successfully with relationships with others.

- Work is most crucial. Whatever work you are occupied with must hold meaning for you.
- Family may also absorb your attention and time.
- You feel in charge of roles or personas that used to control you in the previous decades.
- Your strength comes from embracing a more global view, and understanding that your legacy or contribution can help others.
- Since you fear inactivity and find it difficult to face, it is easy for you to get productive and have some fun.

In these decades, significant relationships are to be found within the workplace, the community, and the family. Usually they revolve around four significant values:

- Companionship and fellowship
- Commitment (There is THAT word again.)
- Caring: concerned, supportive
- Respect: being appreciated

Questions for Review

If you are in your 40s or beyond, take the time to notice the status of your current relationships: make sure to extend your time line to the present. Ask yourself:

- What still needs to change?
- What's working well?
- What's missing?

Know Where You Stand

Love is always bestowed as a gift - freely, willingly, and without expectation...
We don't love to be loved; we love to love.
~Leo Buscaglia

At this point review the developmental tasks and the values that guide these decades and summarize where you are by writing it out in your journal. Are you happy with the result? If not, make a note on how you would like to improve yourself and your relationships. The repair techniques we provide in this book are the stepping-stones to quickly and effectively going from fizzle to sizzle in all of your relationships.

Final Words on Responsiveness

Work with the following statements each day as a reminder to allow intimate conversation and moments of appreciation. You can use the HUG technique to determine which statement you need to work with. Say the statements out loud to yourself and work with them in your journal. One technique we teach is to write the statement at the top of your page then write for 5 to 10 minutes about whatever comes. Allow thoughts and feelings to flow freely. This will help you determine what steps you need to take next.

- I respond by being present.
- Intimacy is not a blame game.
- Conflict, like nature, happens. I deal with it effectively.
- I can decode through intuition the behaviors of those I am in relationship with.
- Authentic relationship is not about making anything go away, it's about acceptance not rejection.
- Resentment and boredom are my enemies. I choose forgiveness and playfulness.
- You know all about me, fully accept me and love me.
- I invite truth in every situation.
- Nobody has a problem; everybody has old emotional patterns.
- Two people create patterns, and one person can change the pattern's dynamics.
- I am willing and ready to change my patterns.
- I take control of myself.
- I choose to lead and quit following.

Remember Mary and Mitch on page82? They worked together to come up with the following list of powerful statements for their relationship:

- We are fully committed to a loving, honest relationship.

- We appreciate and celebrate our relationship.

- We make time to share intimate moments without distractions.

- Whatever happens we can work through it because our love is strong.

Take the time to write positive statements or affirmations for your particular situation. Create the statements that you personally need to work on, that you and your partner want to work on - or even work with your family to clarify what you want to create together. Using powerful statements helps to remind us to shift our mental and emotional state to one of caring and responsiviness.

Successful relationships don't just happen: they are created with intention and practice. Like any other life goal, having a plan in place helps you work through the difficult times with greater ease and sail through the joyful times with sizzling success.

Success is not defined by how you start but by how you continue over time. - Darren Hardy

VI. The Power of Commitment

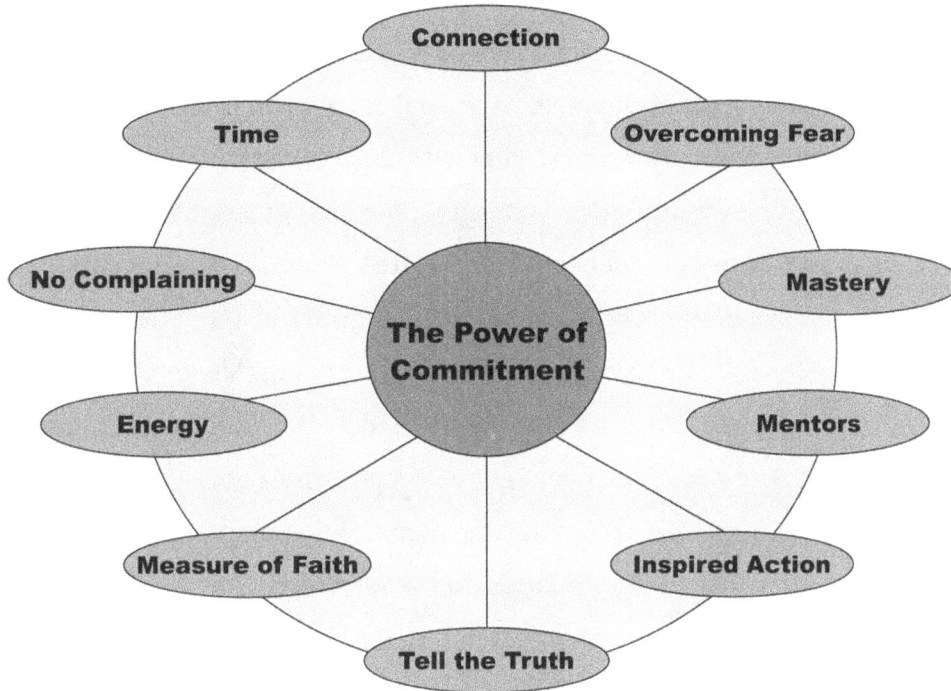

The Wheel of Commitment

We like to think about commitment like a wheel with ten different spokes. If any one of the spokes is broken or out of alignment, the wheel stops rolling. In our work with individuals and couples we have found ten critical areas in our lives that help us understand why we fail to create and sustain the sizzling relationships we dreamed about as teens and young adults. Each spoke on the "Wheel of Commitment" pictured above represents a concept essential to building sizzling relationships. To help you remember these concepts, the first letter of each word combines to spell out commitment.

The reasons why we fail to follow through on our commitments to others and ourselves have to do with our core temperament, our values, and our emotional memories as we have discussed throughout this book. Remember our philosophy: if we can name it, we can tame it.

When you enter into a relationship, especially a romantic relationship, you may not think about commitment on the first date or you may enter into the relationship with trepidation because of the emotional memories tied to commitment issues. In romantic relationships, commitment is often talked about with a capital C. The mere mention of the word can send some people running in the opposite direction or cause others to cling too tightly to a relationship that is no longer working for them.

100

0

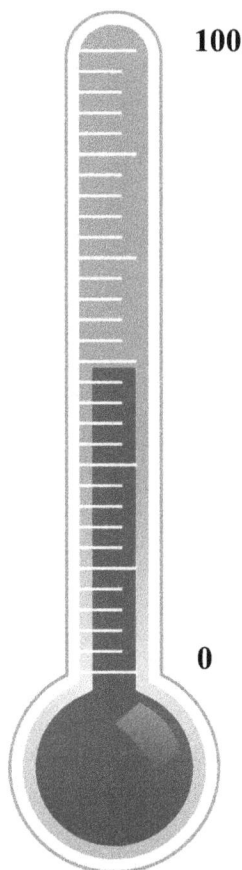

Where are You on the Commitment Scale?

If you are certain that you want to create a sizzling relationship that will stand the test of time and life's interruptions, you must have an honest relationship with commitment. We encourage couples to strive for a soul-level commitment to what you want in your life and in your relationships. A soul-level commitment occurs when you surrender with your whole being, and close all of the back doors and escape routes you have created in your mind. We are not talking about sacrificing individuality or independence: we are talking about committing to the process of engaging in a relationship that delights you every day.

The Latin root of the word "commit" is to bring together and then to send forth. Sounds very much like HUG doesn't it? Finding congruence in our head, heart, and gut before making a commitment is one of the four cornerstones of relationship repair. 99% commitment isn't good enough to sustain a sizzling relationship: you must be 100% committed! Remember the signature to commitment at the beginning of this book? Did you sign it? If not, return now to page 1 and commit. Then mark where you are in your current relationship on the thermometer. This visual reminder will help remind you what action steps in your personal relationships still need to be completed.

Relationships are a process: marriage is a process, raising children is a process, building a business is a process. When we can face the practical realities of life and set aside contemplation of the perfect marriage or the perfect kids, we are free to grow into and with the journey. Everything that we discuss in this book is about understanding the process and being able to consistently realign ourselves to our core temperament, values, and desires.

Connection

Let's start with Connection. On page 40 we discussed connection as one of the most important core values that create sizzling relationships and asked you to think about what you need in order to feel connected to others. As a Bulldozer, you might need intellectual conversation and companionship, but not a lot of romance and hugging. As a Ringmaster, you need adventure, travel with your partner, and lots of creative playtime. For the Detective, you need honesty with your partner and to be with someone who recognizes and acknowledges your efforts. The Border Collie can be a hopeless romantic and values peace in her home and lots of physical affection. You can see how complicated it can be to get your relationship needs met on a consistent basis. Unless you are able to clearly articulate your needs to your partner and to your children, you will feel disconnected, especially if each of you has a different core temperament.

In addition to the need for connection to others, we address an even greater need that must be met first for truly sizzling relationships to happen and endure. That need is a solid connection to self. Once you have identified your core temperament and values, do not just write them down and shut this book. Remember, relationships are a process. The tools offered in this book will help you to create a deeper connection to self and to spirit. The HUG technique is a critical piece of our relationship repair system that you master with consistent practice. Connection ultimately involves the art of listening: to our inner voice, intuition, God, whatever you want to call it that makes sense for you. Listening is half of all communication with self and others. Think again about core temperament: do you need to work on your listening skills?

When we feel disconnected from our self or from our partner, we cannot achieve the soul-level commitment we hope to create and sustain. One of your first challenges in committing to a relationship is to address the issue of connection and its role in your life.

Questions for Review:

Here are several questions related to your ability to connect to self and your need to connect to others for you to review:

- Are you frequently taking the time to listen to yourself?
- What thoughts, feelings or emotions do you need to pay more attention to?
- Are you failing to listen to those around you?
- If you are trying to reach a particular goal/outcome for your relationship, who is connected with your goal? What role do they play?

Overcoming Fear

Fear of commitment usually relates to a series of different fears that a person experiences sequentially or simultaneously that include:

- Fear of getting hurt
- Fear of trusting: that you made the right decision, a certain individual, your ability to succeed
- Fear of not finding the perfect client, partner, business or job

- Fear of not maintaining the illusion of perfection

- Fear of failure related to an individual, relationship, or business/job performance - including pleasing and meeting others' expectations and not letting yourself and others down

- Fear of giving up your identity and independence

We all have fears that stop us in our tracks, but we can usually overcome those fears quickly with the tools we have taught in this book.

Sometimes the fear of commitment is about an outcome you expect to happen. What if you commit to doing something and then the outcome is not what you expected? If you want to deal with this fear, you need to understand that the outcome will never be exactly as you plan it. There will always be slight differences from the way you envisioned it.

Think about what you are most afraid of in your relationship right now. Are you afraid your partner will leave you, laugh at you or ignore you? Be very honest with yourself. In Section V we discussed emotional memories and how they can hijack us along the road to creating our sizzling relationship. Underneath most of our fears is an emotional memory that prevents us from moving forward. Let's look at an example:

Jerry and Margaret came to us because they were having a difficult time communicating what was happening in their relationship and they both felt stuck. During a session, Jerry admitted that he had been angry with Margaret for several months but was afraid to bring it up with her. Margaret had felt Jerry withdrawing from her. He barely spoke to her, wasn't interested in sex, and wouldn't open up to explain to her what was going on. During our discussion, Jerry admitted that he was afraid to tell Margaret how angry he was. His perception of Margaret was that she was very fragile and couldn't handle the strong feelings he was experiencing. Margaret was surprised by this: she did not think of herself as fragile and never worried that Jerry would harm her or yell at her. In fact, after 15 years of marriage, she knew that Jerry struggled with expressing his anger and tended to hold in his feelings until he exploded.

Once they got to the core of what Jerry was angry about, they were able to discuss it calmly and came to realize he had completely misunderstood an argument over finances: he felt Margaret had refused to face the truth of their situation. Margaret was unhappy that it had taken Jerry three months to share this information with her and told Jerry that she was always willing to listen to his feelings and emotions without judgment or fear. After a few more questions we learned that when Jerry was growing up, his Dad did a lot of yelling, causing his Mom to cower and cry in the face of his anger. When he felt his anger rise, he was afraid of making Margaret feel like his Mom.

We asked Jerry and Margaret to outline what a safe conversation would feel like for them. They quickly agreed that Jerry needed a safe outlet for the expression of his anger. For him, that meant a run in a nearby park so he could work out the physical feelings first. Then, they would schedule a time to sit down together to calmly talk things through. Margaret assured Jerry that she was not fragile and felt able to support him in managing his anger, whether it was directed at her or at someone else. Jerry agreed to practice using HUG before these conversations in order to be clear about what he wanted the outcome to be and to be sure his anger was not sparked by an emotional memory but a real feeling about a current situation.

Questions for Review

- When you hear the word "commitment" what pops into your head? Don't analyze it: just write it down. Writing it down will help you see any memories that may be emotionally hijacking your current relationship.
- What are your expectations for a committed romantic relationship? Are they realistic? Do they match your partner's expectations?
- What commitment are you most afraid of right now?

Mastery

Next we'll discuss the concept of mastery as it relates to relationship repair. Mastery means the action or process of mastering a subject, skill, or the accomplishment of a goal. Think about your core temperament: is mastery important to you? If you are a Detective, most definitely, but for a Ringmaster, always learning something new is more important than mastery.

To best accomplish relationship repair you must first master the techniques. As we stated at the beginning of the book, these tools need to be used frequently, repeated often, and practiced on others and ourselves. If you want to be committed to your partner for a lifetime, you will succeed only after you commit yourself to mastering the four core tools taught in this book through practice, practice, practice.

For Dr. Riordan, this level of mastery and achievement is the status quo: she is very self-motivated and driven to succeed. The Bulldozer part of her core temperament often rules her behavior. Her husband and son are more laid back in their approach to life. When her son was younger, she often grumbled to herself about her son doing lots of talking without taking action or completing specific assignments. At school he seemed disorganized and she was sure he could be doing better. He never did any "extra" work and didn't work to perfect his skills in reading and writing. Sitting still to focus on a book or written activity was physically impossible for him. Yet he was making all A's in his classes - why was she worried?

One of his teachers helped Dr. Riordan see that her son had a different core temperament than hers. He is passionate about learning in his own way, engaged in the classroom and very bright. As a 10-year old boy he did not care about reading, writing, or homework. He is the consummate Ringmaster and loves being around people. He needs lots of adventure and physical activity to keep him happy. He thrives in discussions, debates and interactive settings.

Once she understood this, Dr. Riordan learned not to put her need for achievement on the shoulders of her son and to stand back to watch him grow into an amazing young man who is internally motivated in his own way. Now that Dr. Riordan is not focused on his achievements but on his happiness, they argue less and enjoy learning new things together that both are interested in and he loves sharing what he is learning at school with his mom. She realized that the difference in their core temperaments was causing them to approach life from two distinct perspectives. She thought he was not committed to doing well in school but she could not have been more wrong. He was committed, but to learning and interaction, not to grades.

If you are struggling in your relationships, ask yourself if you are mastering the four tools taught in this book through practice, repetition, and acknowledgement of the differences in temperament in your relationships. You cannot say you are committed to creating a sizzling relationship with your spouse, child, friend or colleague if you are not actively improving connection and communication.

Questions for Review:

Here are some questions for reflection around Mastery. Think about these in the context of repairing your relationships (always remember to keep your core temperament in mind as you answer these reflection questions):

- What else do I need to know about my goals?
- Is there something else I need to learn, do or work on?
- Do I have enough information to take inspired action?

Mentors

We want to say a brief word here about finding a mentor. Whether you are looking to repair your relationships with your spouse, child, or boss, it will be challenging to do so alone. While we are teaching you core skills that you can apply to any situation, it is still helpful and necessary to have a safe person in your life that you can talk to you about the situation at hand. We have talked about connection earlier in this chapter and throughout this book: even as adults, we all need at least one person in our lives that we feel deeply connected to and consider safe enough to share whatever challenges we are experiencing. This may be a friend, parent, pastor, coach, or spouse. It is important that you actively cultivate this type of relationship in your life so you quickly become aware that you are not alone in your journey.

Depending on your core temperament, it can be very difficult to ask for help or support from another person. We want to encourage you to use the HUG technique to define what you need from a mentor and who the right person might be. If you are interested in working with a coach or mentor, or would like more information on working with Dr. Goode or Dr. Riordan, visit our Relationship Resource page at the end of the book for details.

If your spouse is normally that person, and you are struggling to recreate the closeness and security you normally experience with him, tell him that. First, check to see what your fears are around the conversation, clear any emotional memories, and create a safe place to have the conversation. Sometimes just telling someone how much you miss him or her can create that safe place to initiate a difficult conversation.

Questions for Review:

If you are looking for a mentor, here are two questions to contemplate:
- Who do I know that can guide/support me in achieving this goal?
- What kind of person do I need to find to help me achieve the desired outcome?

Inspired Action

One of the primary advantages of continued practice with the HUG technique is the increased ability to trust and follow guidance for "inspired action." What is an inspired action and what does it have to do with commitment? It is an action that you take because that little voice in the back of your head or in your heart or in your gut urges you to take it. The more in tune we become with our inner sense of knowing, the more success we will have in repairing relationships quickly and painlessly. Most of us dread confrontation, even if we are the one who is angry: complaining to a girlfriend that we are mad about something our spouse did is easier than telling our spouse we are angry with him.

But what if you listened to that inner voice that guides you to give your spouse an extra hug or to make her lunch as she runs out the door? Perhaps you are guided to stop and buy flowers or a bottle of wine on the way home - or a text saying, "I love you" during the day with no expectation of a return message. All these qualify as inspired actions: they originate within us; we listen, and we act.

Anais Nin wrote, "Our life is composed greatly from dreams, from the unconscious, and they must be brought into connection with action. They must be woven together." Are you spending too much time dreaming of what you want from your relationship, but failing to take action?

Inspired actions are actions we are drawn to take by our inner selves and without any expectation of the outcome. Here is an example.

Dr. Riordan was coaching a business owner, Lorraine, who was struggling with a difficult client. While the client was generating good income for Lorraine's company, he was difficult to communicate with: he had suddenly become less responsive than usual and was not getting the work done that made it possible for Lorraine's team of virtual assistants to accomplish their jobs. There was clearly something out of kilter in the situation and Lorraine was not sure how to progress. In their coaching session, Dr. Riordan asked Lorraine to walk through the HUG technique to determine what she really wanted out of her relationship with this client.

Question	Head Logic-Reason	Heart Emotional Center	Gut Intuitive-practical
Do I want to continue working with this client?	Yes, he brings in money for my business.	I am worried that he is causing stress for my team but we need the money.	I trust him to do the right thing, I need to have a talk with him.
What can I do right now to move towards a solution?	Schedule a call with him for tomorrow.	I need to dig in the garden today to clear my head and prepare for the call.	I want to have a proposal in place to solve this problem before I talk to him.

Lorraine's ultimate desire was to maintain this client and to improve the relationship so that everyone was happy in the work environment. After completing the HUG technique, Lorraine knew exactly what inspired actions she needed to take to move her towards a solution. Lorraine phoned Dr. Riordan later that evening to share her excitement. While digging in the garden, the perfect solution to her communication challenges with the client popped into her head. She realized that her team did not have a suitable way of communicating its needs and deadlines to the client. Lorraine was putting herself in the middle, rather than letting the client and the teams get the job done: she recognized that her need to control the situation was interfering with progress.

Again, you can see how our fears, worries or need to control can interfere in our relationships and stop us from making a soul-level commitment to success. Remember that commitment, just like relationship repair, is a process that takes patience, practice, and the willingness to listen.

Start listening to yourself on a regular basis and when some seemingly whimsical or perhaps more obvious action arises in your mind, do it right away. Not waiting is an important element of successful inspired action. We guarantee that this process works and works fast, especially in your relationships! Remember that we have to take care of ourselves first and stay connected to our core before we can make progress in moving our lives and romance from fizzle to sizzle.

Questions for Review:

- How often do you ask for guidance from self, from Spirit, from your support team of spouse, friends, or coworkers?
- Ask yourself right now: "What is the next step I need to take to deal with _____" We encourage you to answer this question in writing and to keep a record of your inspired actions. Follow up with yourself. Was the outcome what you expected - what you wanted? If not, practice seeing the outcome as positive. Make sure that you are not attached to a specific outcome because of your emotional memories.

Tell the Truth

Here's a story shared by Hannah - a friend of Dr. Riordan's - who struggled with alcoholism for 24 years, when we asked her what commitment meant to her:

What a fascinating word, commitment. I have been committed to many things throughout my life: committed to proving something to my family and society without regard to my own desires; committed to putting on a front that didn't show the pain I felt inside; committed to never ever being alone, therefore jumping from one bad relationship to the next. Commitment shifted for me in 2007, when after 13 glasses of wine and 24 years of being an alcoholic I woke up to the look on the face of my fiancé who had finally had enough. At that moment, he made a commitment to not attach himself to the train wreck I had become.

Today I am committed to awakening to the self that exists inside the alcohol-controlled self that I served for many years. I am committed to me first and that means being compassionate with myself: understanding that I am divine and worthy for no other reason than that I am. I am committed to honoring the gifts, talents, the highs and the lows of the multi-faceted being that I am, to loving this energy called life. Today I understand that we make many commitments in this world but without a commitment to self first, to healing our wounds first, to awakening to our authentic self first, we can do little to heal the world or ourselves.

Commitment is always the unwavering consistent path to something or somewhere – and I am committed to being guided there, trusting that life, the good of all, is committed to me too.

It is human nature to focus our attention and communication on why we CANNOT commit to our clients, business, partner, children, dreams, health, or finances – especially over the long term – and why we waste our energy convincing others and ourselves that our goals are impossible to achieve. In reality this is only a tactic to delay making your soul-level commitment. It took Hannah 24 years to begin to tell herself the truth and to face her reality. Are you telling yourself the truth?

In this section we want to focus on your relationship with yourself and with others. Is honesty high on your values list - but you consistently sabotage your health with overeating or drinking too much alcohol? Is respect high on your list - but you deal with your spouse or your child by screaming at them or retreating from them? Even telling small lies causes an inner shift in your alignment with your values and sense of inner security. People know when you are not being honest with them or even with yourself. What are you hiding from or avoiding by being dishonest? In Hannah's situation, she was hiding from herself because she did not believe it was okay to shine in her own brilliance. She used alcohol to avoid the lies and the discomfort of trying to be someone she was not.

When we are not fully committed, all we see are excuses and we love to share them. We love to rationalize, "Oh just one little French fry - I will starve myself later to make up for it"; "I will get that work-out in tomorrow." By procrastinating, we often ignore the urge to take inspired action. In *Little Orphan Annie* Annie sings, "The sun will come out tomorrow, tomorrow, tomorrow." What about **today**? When we are fully committed and consistently tell ourselves the truth, we see so much more. Suddenly our lives are ripe with possibilities, solutions, and opportunities!

We become more attractive to others when we make a soul-level commitment to ourselves or to something or someone. People sense our enthusiasm and our drive. When we commit to telling the truth in every aspect of our lives, we feel relieved, energized, and refreshed. We are living a congruent life that fills our spirit. It becomes easier to move forward and to take inspired action: we believe in our own ability to make things happen.

Commitment is *SEXY*: people want to share that energy with you!

Questions for Review:

- What excuses am I making?
- What am I lying to myself and others about?
- How can I make it safe to tell the truth?

Measure of Faith

This one is simple and obvious: if you are truly committed to creating a sizzling relationship with your significant other, you have to believe that it can happen. Now that you have all the tools for relationship repair at your fingertips, you have to trust that it will work for you and that you can be the agent of change you want to be. Remember, you are the one who has to change first, to see the world differently and to tell the truth. You must be the role model for what you want to create.

As Joseph Chilton Pearce, author of *Magical Child*, says, "We must become the people we want our children to be." We love this quote: it embodies everything that we are trying to communicate. In any relationship with another human being, we must become who we want ourselves and the other person to be. If you want to be treated with love, do you practice being loving? If you admire honesty and respect, are you honest and respectful in all of your relationships?

It takes "a measure of faith" to step into the position of leader and role model.

Questions for Review:

- On a scale of 1 to 10, how do you rate your faith related to achieving your goal?
- If you are not at a 10, what is one action you can take to move you forward?
- Are you acknowledging and celebrating your small successes along the way? This is a critical step in trusting inspired action, increasing your faith in yourself and continuing to grow.

Energy Management

When our goal is to increase commitment and to create a dynamic, sizzling relationship that fills our heart and soul with joy, we often forget to focus on our energy levels. Learning to manage our energy is a critical component of relationship repair. How you manage your energy may vary according to your core temperament, but it is an area of personal development that needs to be addressed on a daily basis.

When we talk about energy management, we are talking about two key areas of our lives: physical energy and emotional energy. Let's look at each one individually.

Physical energy is derived from our routines for self-care like eating healthy foods, getting enough sleep, getting consistent exercise, brushing our teeth, and bathing. It can also include haircuts, taking care of our nails, and dressing so we feel attractive. You have to care about how you look and feel physically before you can expect anyone else to care. This is not about being physically beautiful or having a muscular body or wearing designer clothes, this is about how much time and attention you dedicate to making yourself feel good. If you are tired, depressed, unhappy with how you look or feel, you will not have the energy to meet the needs of a loved one. Remember, commitment is *SEXY*!

Emotional energy stems from self-confidence and self-worth. Inner strength and beauty are more attractive than external beauty. We have all met people who are charismatic or whose enthusiasm for life is magnetic. For us to be in a positive, romantic and sizzling relationship with another person, we first have to take care of our emotional energy. Are you coming home from work at the end of the day tired, angry, or frustrated? Think about how that energy spills onto your partner or your children, even though you many not intend it to. Some simple ways to get re-centered are to spend five minutes sitting in your car taking deep breaths and naming all the reasons you can't wait to see your family, or asking your family to give you ten minutes of quiet time in the bedroom so you can regroup before joining them for dinner. Perhaps you need physical activity to reenergize you emotionally at the end of the day: so you stop at the gym to work out before heading home.

Let's look at emotional energy and core temperament. Each core temperament manages his or her emotional needs very differently and you need to be aware of this if you are in relationship with someone whose temperament is the opposite of yours.

Bulldozer: Bulldozers have a high tolerance for stress and will often store stress internally for a length of time before they even realize they are suffering. A partner might notice they are quieter or more withdrawn than usual or working longer hours at the office. They ignore their emotions or tend to manage them privately through more work and internal dialogue rather than conversation.

Detective: The Detective manages her emotional energy by trying to solve her problems on her own first by going to her head. She worries, researches and filters through her past memories. She will do research online, write in a journal, read a self-help book, or try to educate herself. It can be difficult for the Detective to reach out and ask for help. Very sensitive in nature, her emotional energy can be drained by too much criticism or if she perceives someone does not value her contribution.

Border Collie: The Border Collie is service-oriented and open-hearted by nature and struggles with his emotions more than other temperaments. He wants to manage his energy by talking through challenges and issues, and needs a supportive listening ear from his partner. The Border Collie becomes depressed when life is not going his way and can be very stubborn when change is required.

Ringmaster: The Ringmaster manages emotional energy by escaping, either to her inner dream world or to an external adventure. Ringmasters may seek out pleasurable experiences, drink too much or drive too fast to feel better. Remember that Ringmasters value freedom and when their emotional energy is drained, they will seek action.

Within the context of your core temperament, are you managing your emotional energy in ways that lead to inspired action and more sizzle? The HUG technique is a powerful tool for managing your emotional energy and ensuring that you stay aligned and congruent.

Questions for Review:

- What are you doing to take care of yourself:
  - Physically?
  - Emotionally?
- What is one thing you can do today or tomorrow to take care of yourself in one of these areas?
- Use HUG to help you understand what is stopping you from caring for yourself. Here are some sample questions you can ask using the HUG technique: "What can I do today to increase my energy?" "Is there an issue I need to address emotionally to be clear for my children?" "What does the pain in my neck need for relief?"

No Complaining!

> *"We have to retrain our thinking and speaking into positive patterns if we want to change our lives." ~Louise Hay*

Complaining is NOT SEXY: the complainer will find it hard to attract friends and you will attract other people who are stuck right along with you. Remember, to reach a soul-level commitment we have to be 100% committed and willing to name and tame whatever it is that holds us back.

We have all experienced the negative energy that comes from being around someone who does nothing but complain, whine, and point out how awful their life and everyone in it is. Have you noticed how easy it is to get pulled into a conversation where you detail all the parts of your life that are going wrong?

All the tools that we have taught throughout this book: core temperament, values, avoiding emotional hijacking, HUG, and following inspired action will help you to recognize this pattern of negative thinking in yourself. The goal is to start focusing on the optimistic. Imagine how your self-image would change if you spent five minutes cataloguing everything that is wonderful about you or describing what you love about your job.

Remember the example of Suzanne and Frank? He had a visceral negative reaction to being regaled with what wasn't working every morning as soon as he got up. She was letting her frustration cloud the precious moment of connection with her husband, connection that she cherished and desired. Just by naming the challenge, this couple was able to tame it and start the morning with a kiss and a snuggle on the couch over coffee.

Questions for Review

- How much energy are you investing in focusing on what is wrong rather than what is right? Take one day and count how many times you judge yourself or others.
- Try spending one day noticing everything that *is working.* Keep a gratitude journal for one week, spending a few minutes every evening making a list of what you were grateful for that day.

Time Management

One of the biggest complaints we hear in relationships is about the lack of time spent on developing the relationship. The truth is, managing our time is just like paying the bills, brushing our teeth, or shopping for groceries once a week. It is a tool and skill that we can develop. In fact, you may have great time management skills at the office, but fail to apply those skills at home.

Commitment takes work: it's about the process, not the outcome. This is not as complicated as it sounds: if you stop, check in with your core values, and remember what is really important, you will quickly learn to restructure your life and relationships in ways that are more meaningful and quickly move you from fizzle to sizzle.

Some examples for improving time management in your relationships might be:
- Scheduling a weekly date for sex with your spouse
- Scheduling a monthly date night out with your partner
- Scheduling a weekly playdate with each of your children
- Scheduling a walk a few times a week
- Implementing a mandatory family dinner night or game night with your kids

If we don't actively schedule time with our spouse and kids, they may fall to the bottom of the to-do list. It may not seem romantic to schedule sex or seem ridiculous to schedule time with your kids who you see every day, but the truth is, we allow other priorities to cloud our true desires. Wouldn't you rather go out to dinner with your wife than fix the back gate?

We encourage you to sit down with your partner and your calendar. See what is filling your time: what can be moved or delegated so that you can carve out more time together? Make sure to write yourselves into your calendar. You have to take these appointments seriously. Miss an appointment? Reschedule it now! Don't wait or the chance for connection will be lost. Creativity is a great tool to employ to make a new routine work for everyone!

Remember that time management mirrors energy management, just as you need to write your spouse and your family into the calendar, you also need to schedule time for self care.

Questions for Review

- Are your action steps, planning time, meditation time, and self-care time written into your calendar?
- Where can you carve out time to work on yourself?
- Are your values reflected in how you are spending your time?

Review

In this section we have discussed ten different areas of our lives that can lead us to leave a little back door open in our minds and stop us from making that soul-level commitment to creating the sizzling relationship that we say we want. When you find yourself struggling with a difficult question or feeling disconnected from your partner, return to this section and run through the ten spokes of the commitment wheel. Use HUG to test your strength and congruence. Are emotional memories hijacking your relationship? Are you afraid of getting too close to someone or of showing your true self? These are questions that roll through our minds in relationships: all you have to do is to name the fears to tame them. Commitment is SEXY: not just commitment to someone else but above all, a soul-level commitment to yourself and to your values. When you are in alignment in your thoughts, feelings, and actions, you act with confidence and enthusiasm: that is *SEXY*!

At the very beginning of this book, you signed a statement saying that you were committing to repairing your relationships - or perhaps you read that part but did not sign it. Now that you have reached this point in the book, read that statement again. Sign the form on page 1 if you have not already. Now you are ready to put your plan of action together.

VII. Bringing Your Intelligent Emotions Into Your Relationships

"You are braver than you believe, stronger than you seem, and smarter than you think."
~Winnie the Pooh

Businesses, couples, and families with children face daunting economic and financial challenges. In tough times you may not act or feel your best. Your expectations clash with the reality of tough times and can cripple any progress towards feeling loved, appreciated, and safe. In tough times you are overwhelmed by a multitude of stresses and you may find yourself reverting to emotional behaviors from your childhood and teen years.

Don't let these circumstances degrade your commitment to yourself and your relationships. We know how easy it is to give up and say:

- "I'll call my sick friend tomorrow."
- "I'll put the kid to bed and veg out on TV."
- "We'll play tomorrow."
- "I have a headache. Sleep well and wake me when you leave in the morning."

Isn't slipping into "I'm tired" easy to do? All of us want to escape and doing so is made easier because the emotional atmosphere at work or at home reflects the turmoil of the greater culture.

Now is the exact time NOT to retreat and hide when you are feeling overwhelmed. Reach deeply into your heart and pull out the strength to move ahead. This is the moment you remember your commitment to an effective relationship with a child, a partner, or a friend. Sometimes your commitment is to yourself, sometimes to the other person in relationship with you, and at other times the commitment is to the *atmosphere* in which the relationship is living, thriving, surviving and existing every day.

What is the Atmosphere of a Relationship?

The atmosphere of a relationship is the emotional space or energy surrounding the relationship, causing it to die, grow, or flourish. The atmosphere can provoke tension, provide comfort, poke at stress buttons, or choke off trust and exchange. The atmosphere promotes coming together or moving apart as reflected in the values that guide your dance between dependence\independence, trust\mistrust, close\distant.

- *Liza was a bulldozer type who drove an hour each way from home to work and back. When she arrived home at 6 pm, her young children steered clear of her as her tension created fear in them. The nanny learned to take the children outside to swing or play so monster mommy had time to drop down into her heart and take a deep breath before nice mommy emerged to hug the kids in a welcoming, not fearful, atmosphere.*

- *Richard, a professional photographer for a popular nature magazine, loved his work and enjoyed taking his two sons (Jeremy, 8, and Jacob, 10) along on photo trips in the Rockies where they lived. Now that Jeremy and Jacob were older, they did not enjoy the trips with their dad like they used to. When they were younger, Dad would talk with them, show them how to identify animal tracks, and camp out periodically. The boys associated these magical trips with Dad as personal time, not work time. Dad had shifted his expectations of the boys as they grew older, telling them to be quiet for longer periods, not camping overnight anymore because he "was working." Dad was blind to the atmosphere he created and couldn't see his boys' desire and need to have fun with him, not sit still as Dad shot photos of animals.*

- *Suzanne is an early riser who loves to get up at 5am and get a couple of hours of work in before her kids and husband get up; then she switches gears to getting everyone ready for the day. She is easily frustrated by computer problems, so there are times when her husband, a computer guru, gets up, walks into her office and immediately gets an earful of what's wrong. Frank is a romantic, loving guy who likes lots of attention and affirmation from his wife. He expects a "Good morning, how are you?" and a kiss when he gets up, not a to-do list.*

Are you **ready** to create an atmosphere that supports you? Are you **willing** to sustain an appropriate relationship with another? Investigating the ways that each of you views the dynamics is helpful, even with children. Here are discussion questions that can help you determine how and what kind of energy and attitude you bring to the emotional atmosphere during an event like an argument:

1. How does each of you perceive what is happening?

2. What is similar in your perceptions? What is different?

3. What are your expectations for the outcome of what is happening?

Similar perceptions imply a better alignment of values, such as those of partners who agree that nature hikes on Sundays start their week on a positive note. Another such agreement would be that a caregiver for a sick parent needs a break, and the parent agrees although she fears being alone. These viewpoints are similar because of shared values like love of nature, need for exercise, or freedom from the tension of stress.

Dissimilar perceptions, which create disagreement, hurtful feelings, or an emotionally toxic atmosphere are most likely caused by core temperament clashes or disparate values. There is no problem with disagreement if it doesn't hinder your ability to discuss topics that affect you and the other person.

What if dissimilar viewpoints cause tension and discord, causing the atmosphere in your home or office to feel heavy, making people want to avoid each other and making it feel unpleasant or full of fear? In such situations, an invitation to change the atmosphere through conversation, new awareness, or action are all helpful. Change needs to happen.

As you assess your core temperament and that of the person in relationship to you, you will learn that you see the world differently. Your perceptions may not gel; you may be unable or unwilling to see another's point of view; your past emotional reactions may rise to the surface to create more distance.

We recommend that you take out your journal and write a description of what you want the atmosphere of your relationships to be - including both your intimate relationship and your relationships with family, coworkers, etc. Write a description for each relationship that you want to change. Knowing what you want to create is one of the first steps to relationship repair. This is a great time to practice using the HUG tool introduced in Section IV. Make sure you are congruent with your desire to create a sizzling atmosphere. These are sample questions for using with the HUG technique:

- "How can I establish a loving atmosphere with my child?"
- "What does my partner need from me for emotional support?"
- "How can I best support my friend right now?"

In Summary

The emotional atmosphere surrounding every relationship between two people is fundamental. How two persons view the atmospheric dynamics and whether you are willing and ready to change the *unsupportive* to *supportive* depends on three factors:

- Cooperation of core temperaments

- Alignment of core values

- Managing emotional reactions

At this point in the book, you should be able to quickly assess how you and another might clash or cooperate in creating an emotional atmosphere that will support and sustain your relationship.

Drip Your Emotional Empathy into the Atmosphere

As the single change agent, you can shift emotional states to change the energy of your emotional atmosphere: every small drop ripples outward.

- Bring your emotional brilliance into the atmosphere and shine some light into those darker areas. The smallest acts make a huge difference – an extra hug, cooking a special dinner, scheduling a date night are some examples.

- A smile when you are tired fuels your energy.

- Movement like walking or dancing changes your energy from tense and quiet to expressive.

- Acknowledging to yourself or the one in relationship to you that your knotted gut can't digest a situation is the first step to acceptance.

- Watching another long enough allows your inner connection to know what the other is feeling. Acknowledge their feelings without judgment or expectation of fixing it: "I can see you are sad, angry, frustrated, etc."

- Admit to feeling personally insecure: naming it is taming it.

- Notice what is going on with your relationship and start a conversation to name it.

All of these reasonable emotional responses reflect your values in a positive light. When you begin to use language that matches your core temperament and values and you notice and respond to the values and temperament of the other person, difficult conversations become much easier to manage. Being out of alignment with your values feels odd – you feel like you are fighting with yourself or are being pulled apart.

When You Can't Breathe

Being in an emotional rut means you see nothing but the walls closing in, soon to suffocate you. Solutions seem far away and you feel alone. How you cope with this suffocating atmosphere is predictable since your response stems from your core temperament.

- The Bulldozer will endure, pushing forward until he blows out and stops.

- The Detective thinks through options, worries, or criticizes.

- The Border Collie frets, withdraws and looks for others who might need help.

- The Ringmaster likes to joke around or find ways to escape from the pressure.

If you want to change the emotional atmosphere, now is the time to notice your knotted gut, headache, or tight neck and shoulders. Now is the time to grow into new awareness: to move past taking it personally and ask someone like a relationship coach, a friend, or your partner for help. In fact, part of the process of maturing into a relationship is acceptance of the person as is; including recognition of how old reactions overtake him or her. Along the way you learn not to take it on yourself or feel personally responsible.

As a member of a baseball team, you have to step up to the plate and try to hit the ball: even if you fail, you still stepped up to the plate. The same is true for the relationship game. You have to step up, take a close look at how you contribute to the emotional atmosphere, and see what adjustments are necessary. How can you tune your emotional response so that it contributes to a positively charged atmosphere and not an explosive one?

Intention, Empathy and Keeping Score

Nurturing the atmosphere of your relationships requires that you bring intention to your relationships. Clearly stating your intentions helps guide your behavior. The following intentions are a good start:

- I intend to ask questions and be open to a conflicting point of view.

- My intention is to stay focused on empathy when we discuss this.

- My intention is to remain aligned with my values and not be swayed.

- I intend to define clear boundaries when I get angry.

Another aspect of intentionality is realizing that communicating in this relational atmosphere with a partner that is unaware of it might require a careful explanation (by teaching or by modeling) of how you want to be treated and spoken to.

Keep in mind that the older you are, the more awareness you need to bring to the table: for instance you may continue to make habitual responses. Try a daily scoring chart to make yourself aware of your limitations. Keep track of how often you have communicated with intention as well as when you have reverted to old habits. Practice saying, "I made a mistake," or "I'll do better if you'll help me or remind me," or "Call it to my attention when I am ranting, will you?" or "Love me enough to tell me I am depressed and help me move out of it."

Other key things to remember while developing this new method of communication include

- Choose to be empathic rather than clinging to the need to be right.

- Choose to be aware rather than withdrawn or alone.

- Be gentle with yourself and your partner. Choosing to change is a practice: don't expect to get it right every time.

- Practice forgiveness! In particualr, forgive yourself and your partner when you fall into old habits.

Head-Heart-Gut™ Responses

In summary, using the intelligence of your emotions to charge up or calm down the relational atmosphere depends upon a proactive stance: "I'm on my side and I am on your side."

- Your inner source of love does not depend upon relationship, but bringing your inner peace into the atmosphere makes a substantial positive contribution. To be in a sizzling relationship with another human being, you must first maintain a sizzling relationship with yourself. We cannot depend on other people to make us happy: we are responsible for our own feelings and our relationships. Our most important relationship is with our self.

- Your personal sense of security assures you will survive and feel safe. If not, you are not in alignment with your values.

- The vast majority of all relationship issues are based on a clash of core temperaments, misaligned values, and reactive emotional patterns. These are in turn influenced by the emotional environment and they can be changed.

HUG responses provide a more positive atmosphere for relationships to grow in intimacy and cooperation. Being still is a HeartWise tool that allows you to scan the atmosphere and know when you are safe and aligned with your values. Your personal energy can affect the atmosphere positively, bringing healing and change.

Being intentional in your relationships and staying attuned to the atmosphere you are creating will help you repair your relationships and turn fizzling relationships into sizzling ones.

You Are the Change Agent

The following guidelines for taking care of yourself in any relationship will help you create long-term, loving connections with others. Only by taking care of yourself first can you have the strength and insight to intentionally create sizzling relationships that thrive and survive the tests of time.

- Love and care for yourself. Your health, attitude, and actions are your responsibility, and the younger you are, the less likely you are to realize this. You blame circumstances, but there will always be changing circumstances. You are the only one who can take charge of the quality of your personal life: after all, you bring YOU to relationships. The two steps which, taken together, change and heal your emotional response patterns are self-acceptance and self-forgiveness. Your journal is a great place to work through issues of self-acceptance and self-forgiveness. See our website at http://www.heartwiserelationships.com for some exercises and journaling questions as well as a guided meditation on forgiveness.

- Next, create in your imagination a greater purpose for your relationship: envision the nature and quality of the loving relationship you wish to create. How does that purpose feel in your heart? Does it bring you joy or make you smile? Does it engender the quality of love that you want? If yes, then you are ready to COMMIT yourself to that higher purpose. If you are ready, then embrace it! Then dedicate that relationship to a higher purpose such as service to others, personal growth and self-development, raising a loving family, or creating prosperity and happiness. Write down your vision in your journal. What we write down has a much higher chance of being successful.

- Share your vision with your partner or children. With your partner or as a family, choose the higher purpose for creating this loving relationship. Commitment is just the first step in fulfilling your higher purpose. Put it in writing.

- The understanding that you have put your clear intention in motion will produce change. Set specific goals for change and commit to taking one action at a time to move you forward. It could be as simple as a date night, a weekend volunteer opportunity, or meditating together.

Ms. Lawrence, a high-end interior designer, hired an assistant, Marianne. According to Marianne, Ms. Lawrence drove her nuts; she barked orders like a dog, gave false compliments, and intimidated Marianne by getting in her face. When Marianne had had enough, she closed her eyes and saw herself scream to her boss that she was leaving; she hated her and hoped never to see her again. Marianne had such strong emotions in her fantasy that her energy overflowed right into the atmosphere of the office. Within 24 hours, Ms. Lawrence fired Marianne: she was free - and not at all unhappy about it.

- Honor change when it happens. People will change and grow differently in their relationship atmosphere. Accommodate the growth: keep the conversation alive and nourish your connection.

- Have fun! Enjoy new experiences and play creatively. What new environment can you explore? Renew playfulness and enjoy each other's company. "Where would you like to go for Sunday brunch?" "Want to go to the beach today?"

Finally, don't be afraid or ashamed to get help. Most of us never learned the "how to" of relationship building. Instead of relying on your old habits, seek out help in learning new ones. Seek help from a trusted parent, friend, or another couple; attend a relationship seminar or seek out a relationship coach. All relationships need a supportive atmosphere so that the people in relationship feel safe and comfortable to express themselves, show love, and receive respect.

VIII. Putting it All Together

In this section, you put all of the pieces together so that you will have both a reminder of what you have learned and a quick summary of your core temperament, your values, your relationship time line, and a place to start a plan of action. You now have all of the tools necessary for relationship repair. It's time to put them to work so that you can enjoy that dynamic, romantic sizzling relationship you are creating.

Assess, Clarify, Review and Repair with HUG

The first step is to assess your personal awareness. You can then use this as a foundation for gauging your relationships. When you understand a factor that drives your reactions, you can name and tame it, change it, and feel completely at peace with yourself.

1. Identify your core temperament so you can go on to define and understand your natural inclination when reacting to people, whether intimates or coworkers, as well as to understand your reactions to stress, tasks and the environment around you. As a reminder of your core temperament, fill out the chart below based on the information from Section II.

2. Discover where those tendencies come from – your childhood environment or current stressful circumstances. Most reactions are simply **emotional memories** from events that happened as you grew up and that have become ingrained within you. Review the emotional memories you discovered working with your defensive behaviors on pages 73-74.

Core Temperament

My primary core temperament is:	
My secondary core temperament is:	
What I have learned about how I react and interact with people is:	

My learning preference is:	
My reaction to stress is:	
My core needs are:	
I take care of myself by:	
What I would like to improve in myself:	

Emotional Memories

Emotional Memory	Defensive Response	HUG Guidance	New Response

Clarify

3. Identify and clarify the values you feel most strongly about. Go back to Section III to review your top ten values and rewrite them in the chart below.

4. Review the relationship profile charts throughout the book to be clear about what you bring to the table as a parent, partner, or a professional. If there are any charts you have not completed yet, do so now.

5. Ask your partner to complete steps one through four. Compare temperaments and values and you will begin to see patterns and instant possibilities for relationship repair emerging that will take you from fizzle to sizzle.

Values

Write a list of your top ten values along with any thoughts for change in the chart below. Use an affirmation in the final column or a suggestion for an activity or goal for increasing that value in your life: see the sample chart on page 51 for ideas.

Value as noun	Value as verb	How to live it
1.		
2		
3.		
4.		
5.		
6.		
7.		
8.		

9.		
10.		

Select one value each week to focus on. Alternatively, use our set of Values Cards to determine what you need to focus on in your life right now. See our Relationship Resources page for details on the set of 52 values cards created by Dr. Riordan to use on a daily basis for your work with defining and acting on your values.

Acting-on-Values Chart

The techniques you can use to put values into action are described in the chart below. This chart is organized as a weekly action log. Each week, as you progress in your relationship repair, you choose your top five values for the week and the people, situations, or events that are most important for you to review. The first several rows are filled in as examples for you.

This chart will help you to achieve three important relationship goals:

1. You will be true to yourself when you base important decisions on being true to your values.
2. You will feel the increase in your self-esteem as you gain confidence. You will recognize that this works and celebrate that progress.
3. You'll not give your power away by saying yes when you mean no, by modeling inappropriate behavior or by allowing yourself not to take care of your own needs.

Acting-on-Values Chart: Sample

Values	Relationahips	Intention	Barrier	CHECK-IN With HUG on Best way to handle the situation	Number of Times I acted on My Intention
Respect	Teenage daughter	To speak calmly, without rancor	She pushes my buttons	Invite her to lunch and conversation. Connect and discuss your emotional hijacking patterns. Ask her to change her comments.	Three, M Th and Sat
Intimacy	Husband	To schedule date night discussion	He works all hours	He needs the break. Persist. He needs you to remind him that you value your time together. Schedule the date.	Successful first discussion tried on Sunday. Was successful on Thursday. Date night for Saturday. Yay.

Acting-on-Values Chart: It's Your Turn

Values	Relationahips	Intention	Barrier	CHECK-IN With HUG on Best way to handle the situation	Number of Times I acted on My Intention

Review

6. Review your life: did you meet the developmental milestones for relationships that all humans pass through? Call to mind your own development in relationships for each decade of your life and add this to your relationship profile.

Based upon your profile, be aware of your reactions the next time you have an emotional flare-up. Chart your emotions on a calendar or in a journal. Note what incidents or emotions sparked the flare-up; start naming them and taming them, one at a time.

Relationship Timeline

If you have not already created your relationship time line, do it now: use a large piece of paper or a blank document on your computer. Write down your relationship history, just like Mary's example on page 81. Doing this will help you see patterns and uncover emotional memories that may be hijacking you today - or it might remind you of what you found sizzling in the relationships of your youth that are missing today.

Repair Using HUG

7. At this point, you know your core temperament(s). You are aware of reactionary emotional memories that might flare up in your profession, parenting, partnership, or friendships. Just like any favorite recipe, relationships get better every time you choose repair and connection. What would you like to repair? List your goals, write down questions about them, and then go get a hug from HUG.

The questions you take to HUG should be straightforward and written clearly. There is no room in your questions for maybe, could, should, what if, and such. Questions that derive clear answers are associated with benefits, best action right now, appropriate actions going forward, best timing, most effective results, clarity, the higher good of all, or what benefits all. The focus is on moving forward with a congruent response from HUG.

Practicing HUG

Reread the instructions on using the HUG technique in Section IV. Pick a relationship challenge you are experiencing right now, using the chart below to record your responses. If they are not congruent, write down one action you can take today to return to inner alignment. Remember, every day this is your go-to formula for keeping the sizzle alive.

Challenge I am having:	
Question I need to ask:	
Head Response:	
Heart Response:	
Gut Response:	

Action step(s):	

8. You make new choices by knowing what you want. Asking HUG questions, considering the answers, and choosing an option to try becomes the model for relationship repair and connection.

Define your sizzling relationship

What a sizzling relationship looks and feels like is different for everyone. Dr. Goode and Dr. Riordan know that the clearer you are about what you want in your life, the easier it is to create. In this section, take the time to describe to yourself a very clear picture of your ideal relationship. Maybe you are in a relationship and want to recapture romance; maybe you are still searching for your soul mate; perhaps you want a better work life or family life.

Write down all the details: what you want, how you want to be treated, how you want to spend your time, where you want to spend your time, etc. Do you love travel or are you a homebody? Be as clear as you can be: use bullet points, doodles, photographs, make a collage, or whatever feels right to you. This is where you have to tell the truth about what you want to create! There is something very powerful about writing your description down. It helps to make it more real in your mind and in your body - forcing you to articulate your dreams makes them clear so that you can attract them effortlessly.

If you name it, you can claim it!

Turn to page 118 and describe your sizzling relationship right now!

Don't wait. This is an important step in the process.

My Sizzling Relationship

This is your space to create exactly what you want!

Action Plan for Making Your Sizzling Relationship a Reality

Now that you have all of the pieces in one place, you are ready to create an action plan: get your calendar out and start planning! Why a calendar? Because it is critically important to write yourself, your goals and your relationships into your calendar. What do you need to add to your calendar? When will you make the time to create your sizzling romance or dynamic family life? Who will you be accountable to: your spouse, friend, child, boss? Use the chart below to create a personal action plan to move you from Fizzle to Sizzle!

Action Needed	To Do	Date to be Completed	Accountable to:	Date actually completed:	Changes in Relationship
Sample: More time alone with spouse - no kids	Find a babysitter Schedule twice monthly date night	Monday of next week Date night 2nd & 4th Sat every month	Husband	All actions completed on time, hooray!	After just one night out alone, we realized we still like each other! And we have more to talk about than our kids.

IX. Final Thoughts

"Today we are faced with the preeminent fact that, if civilization is to survive,
we must cultivate the science of human relationships... the ability of all peoples,
of all kinds, to live together, in the same world, at peace."
-Franklin D. Roosevelt

You should now be well on your way to celebrating all of the changes you have implemented and reaping the benefits of sizzling relationships at home or at work! Rather than giving you more of our thoughts, we'd like to share with you our favorite quotations on relationships to ourselves, each other, and our children. Who better than the sages through the ages and their observations of wisdom to inspire your desire to better your self and your relationships?

When you have moments of doubt, read through this section for inspiration. Need inspiration for your relationship journal? Find it here. Simply write one of the quotes at the top of a blank page and start writing whatever comes as you contemplate the statement.

We have provided you with the science of relationships: core temperaments, management of emotional memories and the wisdom found in the guiding light of your personal values.

Perhaps the most basic, powerful tool for profound relationship repair is the HUG technique for finding, trusting and following your inner truth. Use it to realize that you have everything within you to achieve your desires. Only through experience with HUG do you develop confidence and competence to achieve all you desire in your relationships.

Intimacy & Relationship

"Among men, sex sometimes results in intimacy; among women, intimacy sometimes results in sex."
~ Barbara Cartland

"An intimate relationship does not banish loneliness. Only when we are comfortable with who we are can we truly function independently in a healthy way, can we truly function within a relationship. Two halves do not make a whole when it comes to a healthy relationship: it takes two wholes."
~Patricia Fry

"People are lonely because they build walls instead of bridges."
~Joseph F. Newton

"You meet someone and you're sure you were lovers in a past life. After two weeks with them, you realize why you haven't kept in touch for the last two thousand years."
~Al Cleathen

"Guys are like dogs. They keep comin' back. Ladies are like cats. Yell at a cat one time, they're gone."
~Lenny Bruce

"Let us be grateful to people who make us happy, they are the charming gardeners who make our souls blossom."
~Marcel Proust

"Some of the biggest challenges in relationships come from the fact that most people enter a relationship in order to get something: they're trying to find someone who's going to make them feel good. In reality, the only way a relationship will last is if you see your relationship as a place that you go to give, and not a place that you go to take."
~Anthony Robbins

"Relationships are the hallmark of the mature person."
~Brian Tracy

"People change and forget to tell each other."
~Lillian Hellman

"Sometimes you have to get to know someone really well to realize you're really strangers."
~Mary Tyler Moore

"You cannot be lonely if you like the person you're alone with."
~Wayne W. Dyer

"The more connections you and your lover make, not just between your bodies, but between your minds, your hearts, and your souls, the more you will strengthen the fabric of your relationship, and the more real moments you will experience together."
~Barbara De Angelis

"If you were going to die soon and had only one phone call you could make, who would you call and what would you say? And why are you waiting?"

~Stephen Levine

"Don't smother each other. No one can grow in the shade."
~Leo Buscaglia

"Assumptions are the termites of relationships."
~Henry Winkler

"You can kiss your family and friends good-bye and put miles between you, but at the same time you carry them with you in your heart, your mind, your stomach, because you do not just live in a world but a world lives in you."
~Frederick Buechner

"Present your family and friends with their eulogies now - they won't be able to hear how much you love them and appreciate them from inside the coffin."
~Anonymous

Relationships With Children

Always kiss your children goodnight - even if they're already asleep.
~H. Jackson Brown, Jr.

Your children need your presence more than your presents.
~Jesse Jackson

It's not only children who grow. Parents do too. As much as we watch to see what our children do with their lives, they are watching us to see what we do with ours. I can't tell my children to reach for the sun. All I can do is reach for it, myself.
~Joyce Maynard

Don't worry that children never listen to you; worry that they are always watching you.
~Robert Fulghum

If you want children to keep their feet on the ground, put some responsibility on their shoulders.
~Abigail Van Buren

The quickest way for a parent to get a child's attention is to sit down and look comfortable.
~Lane Olinghouse

If there is anything that we wish to change in the child, we should first examine it and see whether it is not something that could better be changed in ourselves.
~C.G. Jung

Don't handicap your children by making their lives easy.
~Robert A. Heinlein

Too often we give children answers to remember rather than problems to solve.
~Roger Lewin

Simply having children does not make mothers.
~John A. Shedd

Although there are many trial marriages... there is no such thing as a trial child.
~Gail Sheehy

Do not ask that your kids live up to your expectations. Let your kids be who they are, and your expectations will be in breathless pursuit.

~Robert Brault

Each day of our lives we make deposits in the memory banks of our children.
~Charles R. Swindoll

What a child doesn't receive he can seldom later give.
~P.D. James, Time to Be in Earnest

If you want your children to improve, let them overhear the nice things you say about them to others.
~Haim Ginott

Kids spell love T-I-M-E.
~John Crudele

The guys who fear becoming fathers don't understand that fathering is not something perfect men do, but something that perfects the man. The end product of child raising is not the child but the parent.
~Frank Pittman, Man Enough

When my kids become wild and unruly, I use a nice, safe playpen. When they're finished, I climb out.
~Erma Bombeck

Parents who are afraid to put their foot down usually have children who step on their toes.
~Chinese Proverb

Instant availability without continuous presence is probably the best role a mother can play.
~Lotte Bailyn

What's done to children, they will do to society.
~Karl Menninger

Friendship

A single rose can be my garden... a single friend, my world.
~Leo Buscaglia

In everyone's life, at some time, our inner fire goes out. It is then burst into flame by an encounter with another human being. We should all be thankful for those people who rekindle the inner spirit.
~Albert Schweitzer

If a friend is in trouble, don't annoy him by asking if there is anything you can do. Think up something appropriate and do it.
~Edgar Watson Howe

The most beautiful discovery true friends make is that they can grow separately without growing apart.
~Elisabeth Foley

A friend knows the song in my heart and sings it to me when my memory fails.
~Donna Roberts

True friendship comes when silence between two people is comfortable.
~Dave Tyson Gentry

A friend is the one who comes in when the whole world has gone out.
~Grace Pulpit

Self-Love

The degree to which you love yourself will determine your ability to love the other person, who will be reflecting back to you many of your own personality traits and qualities.

~Sanaya Roman

When you are compassionate with yourself, you trust in your soul, which you let guide your life. Your soul knows the geography of your destiny better than you do.

~John O'Donohue

The voice within is what I'm married to. All marriage is a metaphor for that marriage. My lover is the place inside me where an honest yes and no come from. That's my true partner. It's always there.

And to tell you yes when my integrity says no is to divorce that partner.

~Byron Katie

Love brings you face to face with your self. It's impossible to love another if you cannot love yourself.
~John Pierrakos

Self-love is the foundation of our loving practice. Without it our other efforts to love fail. Giving ourselves love we provide our inner being with the opportunity to have the unconditional love we may have always longed to receive from someone else.

~bell hooks

"When you're different, sometimes you don't see the millions of people who accept you for what you are. All you notice is the person who doesn't."

~ Jodi Picoult

The only person who can pull me down is myself, and I'm not going to let myself pull me down anymore."

~C. JoyBell C.

"Letting ourselves be forgiven is one of the most difficult healings we will undertake. And one of the most fruitful. (79)"
~Stephen Levine,

You, yourself, as much as anybody in the entire universe, deserve your love and affection.

~Buddha (563 - 483 BC)

Love & Life

"I love you not only for what you are, but for what I am when I am with you. I love you not only for what you have made of yourself, but for what you are making of me. I love you for the part of me that you bring out."

~Roy Croft

"True love stories never have endings."

~Richard Bach

"In this life we cannot do great things. We can only do small things with great love."

~Mother Teresa

"What most people need to learn in life is how to love people and use things instead of using people and loving things."

~Author Unknown

About the Authors

Dr. Caron Goode, NCC

Dr. Goode is the founder of the HeartWise relationship strategies involving alignment through head-heart-gut, which she now shares in her co-authored new book <u>From Fizzle to Sizzle, 4 Crucial Tools for Relationship Repair.</u>

Dr. Goode is the founder of the Academy for Coaching Parents International, where professionals and parents become ACPI Certified Parenting Coaches\Consultants and learn to use the HeartWise coaching strategies with their coaching clients and in their business.

Dr. Goode and her husband, Dr. Tom Goode, also train professionals, especially those with affective or intuitive core temperaments in the Heart-Wise alignment process (a.k.a.- HUG) in addition to training and certifying Intuitive Consultants who bring HeartWise strategies into their professional business or practice. HeartWise Parenting strategies offer connection and responsiveness to meet our children's needs and encourage their core strengths for well-rounded life experiences.

Dr. Goode features her classes for sensitive, empathic, and spiritual people at the http://Live-Spirit.com learning center. Dr. Goode is the author of fifteen books and more than a dozen e-books and trains others in coaching skills, marketing plans to monetize passion, and the use of intuition in parenting, business, living and loving.

http://AcademyforCoachingParents.com

http://Live-Spirit.com

http://HeartwiseParent.com

http//:www.Fizzle2sizzle.com

http://www.HeartWiseRelationships.com

Dr. Minette Riordan, ACPI CPC

Dr. Minette Riordan is co-author of the book <u>From Fizzle to Sizzle: Four Crucial Tools For Relationship Repair</u>. Minette's passion for connecting people to each other is deeply rooted in her belief that it is our connection to spirit, to self and to others that is the foundation of true happiness. Over the years, Minette has found many unique ways of

helping people to create both inner connection to their higher self and powerful connections to others around them. Through Minette's work as a teacher, writer, speaker, artist, community volunteer and an award-winning business owner, she has educated thousands of people on the subjects of communication, commitment, and connection.

Dr. Goode and Dr. Riordan met in 2006 when Dr. Riordan became certified as a Parenting Coach through the Academy for Parent Coaching International. Minette quickly moved from trainee to trainer and now teaches for ACPI. In addition to her work with ACPI, Dr. Minette Riordan successfully built a multi-media publishing company targeting families in the Dallas/Ft. Worth Metroplex. She credits her success to learning how to connect with others through networking, referrals, strategic partnerships and an attitude of service to others first. Minette's secret to success is not about winning a numbers game, but playing the people game: cultivating an attitude of curiosity and openness that will quickly help you attract clients and fans.

Dr. Riordan is a dynamic public speaker who excels at engaging and entertaining her audiences. She also workshops, retreats and individual coaching programs. You can find out more about her speaking and programs at http://www.minetteriordan.com

Prior to starting her company, Minette was an educator who earned her Ph.D. from Stanford University in 1995. She has taught at the university and high school levels, as well as adult education and personal development workshops. In 2011 she received the Libby Linebarger Award from the Texas Home Childcare Association. She was named the 2009 Small Business Owner of the Year by the Plano Chamber of Commerce and received the 2007 Altrusa Outstanding Women of Today award.

Her passion and joy come from helping others find the information, tools and inspiration they need to succeed. She is living proof that you can have it all: a successful business, healthy marriage and happy kids! Minette lives in Santa Barbara, California with her husband, Brad and her two children, ages 13 and 10.

Dr. Riordan offers workshops and individual coaching for women. You can find more at:
http//:www.MinetteRiordan.com
http://www.HeartWiseRelationships.com

Relationship Resources from HeartWise™

Dr. Caron Goode and Dr. Minette Riordan offer a variety of educational workshops, webinars, and teleseminars as well as individual and group coaching programs to help you get from fizzle to sizzle in your relationships. You can learn more about all of our programs on our website at http://www.heartwiserelationships.com. You can purchase additional copies of the book at http://www.Fizzle2Sizzle.com.

Here is a sample of the online programs we offer for Relationship Repair:

- Know your Core 4 - An Introduction to Core Temperaments and Why they Matter
- How Core Values Add Meaning and Focus to your Life
- Stop the Emotional Hijacking Now! How to Identify and Change the Defensive Behaviors that Hold You Back
- Learn to HUG Yourself: How to Apply Head-Heart-Gut to your Daily Life

Certified Intuitive Coach Training

Love the HUG tecnhique? Consider Dr. Goode's Certified Intuitive Coach Training. Learn to use the technique more effectively in your own life and learn to use it with others. If you are a coach, educator, therapist or healer, the HUG technique is a great addition to your toolbox. You will be able to quickly get to the core of what is happening with your clients and help them take the right action to move forward fast. For more information on the Intuitive Coach Training, visit http://www.live-spirit.com

Certified Relationship Coach Training

Interested in becoming a Certified Relationship Coach using Dr. Goode and Dr. Riordan's tools as describe in this book? Ask us about our Train-the-Trainer program.
Visit http://www.heartwiserelationships.com for more information.

Additional Resources

Access to additional information and all of the resources and downloadable files mentioned in From Fizzle to Sizzle can be found on http://www.heartwiserelationships.com. HeartWise™ Values Cards

Living a values-based life is equivalent to living a HeartWise™ life. When we honor our core values, decisions are easier to make, life is more fulfilling and relationships are less troubled. This deck of 52-values cards are designed to help you focus on the core values that are most important to you or that you need to pay more attention to in order to live a heart-centered life. They are also a great tool for families and couples who want a fun, creative way to talk about core values. These cards are an invitation to live a HeartWise™ life that is joyful, authentic and intentional.

For information on ordering the cards, please visit http://www.heartwiserelationships.com.